The Book of Over-Thinking

Gwendoline Smith is a clinical psychologist, speaker, blogger and the author of the books *The Book of Knowing, Depression Explained* and *Sharing the Load*. She also goes by the name Dr Know. Born and raised in Chatham, Kent, she now lives in Auckland, New Zealand.

The Book of Over-Thinking

How to Stop the Cycle of Worry

Gwendoline Smith

ALLEN&UNWIN

First published in Australia and New Zealand in 2020 by
Allen & Unwin.

First published in Great Britain in 2021 by Allen & Unwin,
an imprint of Atlantic Books Ltd.

10 9 8 7 6 5 4 3 2 1

A CIP catalogue record for this book is available from the British Library.

Paperback ISBN: 978 1 83895 278 5
E-book ISBN: 978 1 83895 279 2

Text design by Megan van Staden
Illustrations by Georgia Arnold, Gabrielle Maffey and Megan van Staden

Printed in Great Britain

Allen & Unwin
An imprint of Atlantic Books Ltd
Ormond House
26–27 Boswell Street
London
WC1N 3JZ

www.allenandunwin.com/uk

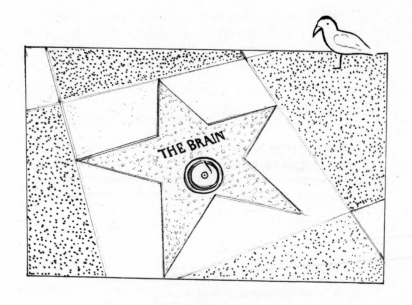

Dedicated to the brain—

for without mine, I couldn't help yours

CONTENTS

If you've just picked up this book, I'm working on the assumption that overthinking is causing you a few problems.

If it is, then you're in exactly the right place.

AUTHOR'S NOTE

The Book of Overthinking is essentially a sequel to my earlier book, _The Book of Knowing_. Both books are grounded in the theory of cognitive behavioural therapy (CBT), recognised as the state-of-the-art treatment methodology for mood and anxiety conditions.

The most important emphasis of this approach is to teach people about _how_ they think, and in doing so provide tools and strategies to better manage how they feel. The focus of _The Book of Knowing_ was to address the needs of teens and young adults, struggling with the overwhelming feelings which we know have a direct link to ever-increasing youth mental health problems. Although it was pitched to younger people, the content was, and still is, helpful to people of all ages.

In my clinic I have seen the magic of *The Book of Knowing* change the lives of many young people for the better. What I have also become aware of in my clinical life is that the majority of adult clients I see are struggling with worry or, as it is commonly known, 'overthinking'.

Hence, *The Book of Overthinking* is geared more to adult readers, though, as was the case with *Knowing*, the knowledge and practical techniques are ageless.

I enticed my lovely illustrators Gabi and Georgia and designer Megan into doing another book with me, as I believe grown-ups love comic books as much as kids do. So have a laugh and learn along the way.

PART 1

WHAT IS OVER-THINKING?

CHAPTER ONE

OVERTHINKING: A DEFINITION

---

overthink (verb)
to think too much about
(something): to put too much time
into thinking about or analysing
(something) in a way that is more
harmful than helpful. (*Merriam-
Webster online dictionary*)

Out of the many definitions I found of overthinking, I warmed to this one the most, because it describes the act in very simple terms. It also highlights the potential to be harmful that overthinking has.

Everyone overthinks things once in a while. However, there are those individuals—perhaps you are one of them—who find it quite impossible to shut down the constant onslaught of unwanted thoughts. There are two distinct forms of this type of inner monologue:

1. Ruminating, which involves rehashing the past.
   - I shouldn't have made that comment in the meeting last week.
   - I shouldn't have left my last job. If I had stayed, I would be much happier than I am now.
   - I shouldn't have eaten that piece of cake at the party yesterday. Now I am going to be fat forever.

These thought patterns are closely associated with regret and guilt.

2. Worrying, which is when you consistently make negative, catastrophic predictions about the future.
   - When I hand in my report to the boss, she will think it is hopeless and then I will be handed my notice. Then I won't be able to pay my mortgage, I'll lose the house and won't be able to provide for my family.
   - And so on, and so forth.

Worrying about potential future disasters creates fear and anxiety.

Being plagued by either or both of these types of overthinking can leave you in a state of constant anguish.

On a lighter note, it is our ability to think that makes us human. It is natural to get absorbed by what we are doing and think about those things. However, if overthinking leads you into a downward spiral of negative, destructive thoughts then, 'Houston, we have a problem.'

Once this process occurs, you begin to create problems that aren't there. Subsequently, you begin to believe and feel that those problems are real and valid. As a result of these beliefs, you then begin to worry and feel anxious. The thoughts then become paralysing, and impede your ability to problem-solve.

The other definition of overthinking which I like comes from the online *Urban Dictionary*:

Not too far off the mark, I say!

All jokes aside, however, I believe that the more knowledge you have about what you are experiencing, the closer you are to managing those unwanted thoughts and experiences.

SHOULD I BE CONCERNED ABOUT MY OVERTHINKING?

People often ask me if all overthinking is harmful. In my opinion, no. Sometimes we can become engrossed in thought, and be stimulated by that experience—like we have been hypnotised, losing track of time in an almost trance-like state. I guess we could liken this to daydreaming or mind-wandering.

Here are a few examples:

You have just fallen in love, and you find yourself thinking about that person all day. You may even dream about them at night. (I guess that's day- and night-dreaming.)

Is that problematic? No. Most people love that experience and find it enjoyable and exciting, not anxiety-provoking.

Your wedding is coming up. You want your hair and dress to be just right, so you think about options and colours all day.

Is that a problem? It can't be that bad—a lot of people appear to keep getting married, and surviving it!

You're training for a swimming competition, and you think about your strokes and your breathing constantly.

Problem? Sounds more like a desire to succeed. Athletes live in this psychological domain through-out their careers. It is only when this thought pattern is driven by a fear of failure (and turns into worry) that sports psychologists intervene.

You find yourself constantly thinking about your golf swing or the new recipe you are going to try when your friends come for dinner. Thinking and planning, thinking and planning.

Problem or excitement? I suggest the latter.

The answer lies in *how* you are thinking. If your thinking goes like this:

OMG I've chosen the wrong colours for the bridesmaids. I'm going to look fat in my dress. I should have got the A-line vintage dress and not the chiffon meringue. People are going to think 'Why is he marrying that fat cow with no dress sense?'

These are the types of thoughts that will create fear and produce toxic over-stimulation.

But if the thinking goes like this:

I am so looking forward to my wedding day. My girls are going to look gorgeous, and so will my hubby-to-be. I love my dress, I love the invites, the venue is perfect . . .

This kind of thinking is pleasurably stimulating, even though you may think about the same topic

throughout the day and into the night. Over-thinking, yes—but a problem? I don't think so.

One of the things about overthinking that clinicians get concerned about is if it is disturbing your sleep. If you spend all night thinking about your bridesmaids' dresses, does that make it a problem?

Not necessarily. You will probably be exhausted the following night and drift off to sleep with ease, so you have not established a pattern of poor sleep. But fear-based overthinking can create chemicals in the brain that are unhelpful to the system, and result in disturbed sleep.

What I will refer to as **positive overthinking** activates chemicals in the brain such as dopamine, oxytocin, serotonin and endorphins—all associated with happiness. This means we desire them and, in the extreme, will repeat behaviours that assure access to them. Humans seek endorphin stimulation via exercise, watching comedy, listening to music, engaging in creative pursuits and so on.

However, when the pursuit of pleasure involves behaviours that provide a means to avoid life's daily problems—e.g. gambling, watching screens, using gaming machines and drinking alcohol—it is not so harmless. (At a conference on compulsive gambling I went to many years ago, the keynote speaker said that the difference between a recreational gambler and a compulsive gambler is that the addict is looking to solve problems through their gambling. This is in contrast to the recreational punter, who is looking for a flutter, a bit of excitement and a night out.)

As you can see from the examples above, not all overthinking is positive. Now let's take a look at **negative overthinking**. Studies show that getting stuck in your head, focusing on negative events (and therefore experiencing feelings of regret, self-blame), can be the biggest predictor of some of todays' most common mental-health problems, such as anxiety and depression. These studies— of which there are millions—introduce us to and educate us on the detrimental health impacts of negative overthinking.

So, the question 'Should I be concerned about my overthinking?' has a simple answer:

'Yes, if it is thinking that gets in the way of your ability to function.'
—DR ROBERT SHIEFF, PSYCHIATRIST AND
COGNITIVE BEHAVIOURAL THERAPIST

CHAPTER TWO

THE HARMFUL ASPECTS OF OVERTHINKING

In the clinical world, we are faced with many differing types and forms of what would generically be labelled 'overthinking'. Overthinking is a popular topic. Dr Google gives you a choice of 24,700,000 listings! (I may add that Googling is also a very popular pastime for the negative overthinker.)

In the process of writing this chapter, I found myself Googling for hours, overthinking the definition of overthinking. Is it positive or negative? Is it worry or is it rumination? Are worry and overthinking the same thing, or are they different, or maybe a little bit the same? Am I overthinking? Yes. As you have read in the previous pages, these things are all inseparably linked.

Overthinking, like so many other clinical terms, has become absorbed into everyday usage. So when you ask people, including my colleagues and clients, whether overthinking and worrying are the same thing, most of them consider the two things

to be 'the same but different'. Sometimes it's a combination of bits of one and bits of the other. For example:

I can overthink and it's fine, then I start to worry. Then I get anxious and then I get worried about being anxious, and then I start to overthink everything and ruminate about what I have been doing and get anxious about what I'm going to do next.

I'm going to make it easier for you—and me, for that matter—and dig myself out of this predicament by describing this complex psychological phenomenon as **worrisome overthinking**. I think you'll agree that this term covers most of the bases.

Clinicians tend to concentrate on and label overthinking as rumination, defined as 'the focused attention on the symptoms of one's distress, and on its possible causes and consequences, as opposed to its solutions'.

They also acknowledge the relationship between overthinking and anxiety as a union of devilish partners.

HEALTH ANXIETY: AN EXAMPLE

A classic example of this is health anxiety (which used to be known as hypochondria). 'Worrisome overthinking' is the dominant thinking style in health anxiety, but in this instance the focus is on everything to do with health.

It goes a bit like this . . .

You're getting ready in the morning and are just about to clean your teeth. You floss first, as is your way, and a small amount of blood appears. You send your tongue on a fact-finding mission around your mouth and notice a small lump-like thing. You start to worry—instant feelings of anxiety appear. With a bit of time up your sleeve before you head out into the traffic, you rush to Dr Google for reassurance.

Enter: *gum disease*. OMG! 103,000,000 results!

Too huge! Narrow the search—quickly, narrow the search.

Enter: *gum cancer*. Only 37,500,00 results—a bit more accessible. OK, scroll down to signs and symptoms.

Warning signs and symptoms of oral cancer: difficulty chewing or swallowing. A lump or sore area in the mouth, throat or on the lips. A white

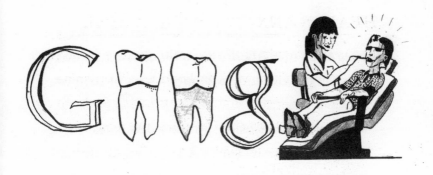

or red patch in the mouth. Difficulty moving the tongue or jaw.

There it is in black and white—the worst possible outcome! Checking your mouth again, as you have been for the past 30 minutes or so, you *do* have a sore area on your gum from where your tongue has been agitating the gum surface. It's time for a trip to the doctor to confirm your worst fears.

When people feel anxious, their main goal is to shift the anxiety so they can feel better. Certainly the lump (or perceived lump) on the gum is an issue, but the main concern is to shift the feelings of anxiety. People with health anxiety spend a lot of money on medical examinations and varying tests, to gain reassurance.

The doctor examines you and proclaims everything to be fine—there's just a bit of agitation from your tongue vigilantly exploring. A bit of soothing gel will do the trick.

Whew, what a relief ! Anxiety dissipates—for a little while, anyway. Then the 'worry warts' are back on the job and off you go again—more worry, more anxiety.

Author's note: Beware of
reassurance-seeking!
The message here is that you have
to learn to reduce your own anxiety.
Relying on other people will only
provide you with short-term relief.

All the academic ins and outs about overthinking don't really matter that much. The main focus is on reconstructing your current thinking to be more helpful and reality-based. That way you get to feel more comfortable in your own skin.

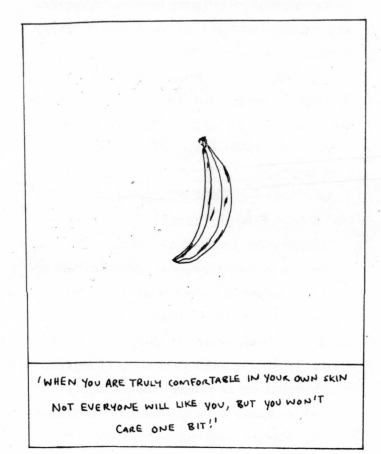

"WHEN YOU ARE TRULY COMFORTABLE IN YOUR OWN SKIN NOT EVERYONE WILL LIKE YOU, BUT YOU WON'T CARE ONE BIT!"

HOW THE BODY RESPONDS
TO OVERTHINKING

Compared to positive overthinking, negative or worrisome overthinking creates a very different chemical reaction in the body. This type of overthinking activates the production of adrenaline and cortisol, the stress hormones. These are the chemicals (hormones) associated with fear.

The body's natural fight/flight/freeze response (survival response) unleashes these powerful hormones, skyrocketing your heart rate and blood pressure and causing other physical sensations, illustrated opposite.

All of these responses can be switched on by just *one* fearful (worrisome) thought.

The body's production of adrenaline in response to fear is a response which has evolved to help us survive. If our ancient ancestors were startled by a noise in the undergrowth, they would either attack (fight), run away (flight) or stay very, very still (freeze). When adrenaline kicks in, your body sends more blood to your extremities (e.g. legs) and less to the stomach (suppressing appetite and causing that butterfly feeling in your gut). This means you run

SURVIVAL RESPONSE

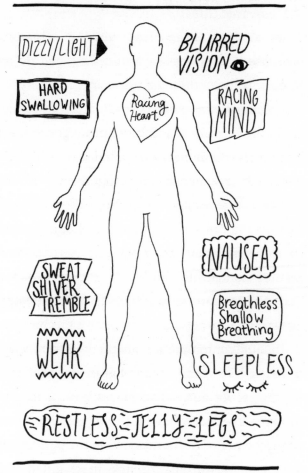

DIZZY/LIGHT

BLURRED VISION

HARD SWALLOWING

Racing Heart

RACING MIND

NAUSEA

SWEAT SHIVER TREMBLE

Breathless Shallow Breathing

WEAK

SLEEPLESS

RESTLESS JELLY LEGS

FIGHT/FLIGHT/FREEZE

Some of the physical reactions that can occur
as part of your body's 'survival response'—
preparing you to fight, flee or freeze.

faster and become physically stronger, to deal with the perceived threat.

In ancient times, fear was an appropriate response. Our ancestors would have had no time to establish whether the noise in the bushes was something harmless or a potentially life-threatening situation (e.g. snake, sabre-tooth tiger, or some other carnivorous creature from Jurassic Park). Fear was absolutely necessary for our survival!

However, because a feeling of fear is our natural response to a rush of adrenaline, as soon as we experience the associated sensations we assume something terrible is about to happen. Today, adrenaline is interpreted as an indicator of catastrophe, rather than a protective mechanism.

In our contemporary jungle it is our way of thinking, our mind, our imagination, that create the trigger for adrenaline production. It might be thinking about not having the biggest house, or a wardrobe full of fashion labels, or the perfect body, the most prestigious car, the most gifted child. These beliefs are mistaken for real-life threats, even though we know that **beliefs are not facts**.

In these situations, upon experiencing the

emotion of fear, the physical bodily sensations caused by adrenaline result in us predicting real danger—even though this 'fear' is self-created (imagined) and not based on any factual evidence of a life-threatening circumstance.

Something else worth mentioning is that when the fight/flight/freeze mechanism is switched on, you are being geared up to flee or fight. For instance:

Imagine you are in your study playing a game of chess with a friend. The smoke alarms are screaming, smoke is billowing in under the door and the kitchen is on fire—but you make the call to continue the chess game.

Yeah, right! The ability to think rationally about your next chess move is not a priority for Mother Nature. What you would actually do is utilise all of your adrenaline-fuelled super-strength and head for safety—however you can, and whatever it takes.

> Remember, this response is not
> a bad thing. Adrenaline is a
> natural reaction to threat. It's
> actually there to protect us.

The problem is when this mechanism continues to be in operation over long periods of time, constantly switching the alarm system (fight/flight) on and off. Over time this will begin to take a toll on your overall health and wellbeing.

For example, you may start to experience:

- bowel problems
- stomach ulcers
- muscle tension
- headaches
- sleep disturbance
- fatigue.

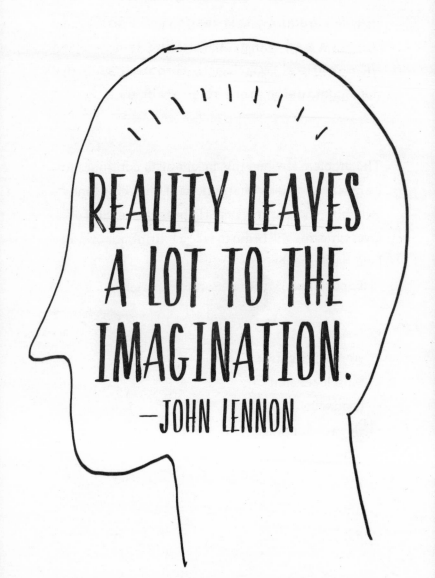

REALITY LEAVES
A LOT TO THE
IMAGINATION.

—JOHN LENNON

It is important to understand that it is worrisome overthinking, in conjunction with your imagination, that creates this fear and anxiety, leading to the adrenaline response.

CHAPTER THREE

A CLOSER LOOK AT THE MECHANICS OF WORRISOME OVERTHINKING

The model opposite was devised by Dr Aaron Beck, the 'father' of cognitive behavioural therapy (CBT). It is brilliant for describing and illustrating many of the aspects of the negative impact of worrisome overthinking, across all fronts: biological, behavioural, emotional and cognitive (thinking). It also provides the template for treatment, as you will see later in the second part of the book.

BIOLOGY

I'm going to start with this sphere of the model, as the biological contribution to anxiety (a by-product of worrisome overthinking) is not something that many people are aware of.

Genetics and family history (e.g. parental anxiety) may increase the risk of someone suffering from an anxiety disorder. Theorists estimate a genetic influence of between 25 and 40 per cent

The cognitive behavioural therapy (CBT) model.

(depending on the specific type of anxiety and the age group being studied).

Without getting too neuroscientific, 'state anxiety' is the experience of unpleasant emotional arousal in the face of threatening demands or danger. For many people this experience is transitional and subsides in a relatively short period of time—anxiety is an alarm system, after all.

An individual with a genetic predisposition to 'high trait' anxiety, on the other hand, will experience a more intense degree of state anxiety, with each incident taking longer to resolve.

I often use the following example to illustrate this complex combination of genetic and environmental factors in anxiety.

Think back to when you were a child. Imagine it's a sunny day, and you are out playing with your friend in the front garden when a very excited neighbourhood dog decides he wants to join in.

Both you and your friend are startled and start to squeal nervously. The owner of the dog comes over to apologise, and reassures you both that the dog is very friendly and loves children—he just wants to

play. Then off they go, leaving you and your friend to continue with your game.

However, the difference between you and your friend is that your buddy calms down fairly quickly and is not really affected by the experience. (Only reaching, say, 60 out of 100 units of distress, 100 being the most anxious you have ever felt.)

You, however, with 'high trait' anxiety, are still experiencing a racing heart, shallow breathing and other fear-related sensations, having peaked at 90/100 units of distress. Your fear feels more intense and takes longer to resolve.

The next time you and your friend see that dog— or any dog, for that matter—it looks like this:

Your friend

You

The experiences are very different and the memories are different. Ingrained in your memory is the distress that you felt. Hence, you develop a fear response, wanting to flee from the stimulus. Your friend, unfazed, can't wait for a bit of rough and tumble with the friendly, playful dog.

I like this example, as it also gives you a brief insight into the development of phobias. It is the *experience of fear* that you remember—whether it was a dog, a spider, a rat, a seagull . . . doesn't matter.

A BIT MORE NEUROBIOLOGY

A lot of people ask me: 'How come when I am feeling irrational, I just feel as though I have no control?'

Well, that is best explained by looking at the two systems in our brain that are most involved with our responses to the world:

1. Limbic system

This is often referred to as the emotional system (the *irrational* part of the brain, for our purposes). It is a set of structures deep within the brain that activate in situations that threaten our survival and wellbeing.

Under threat, a little structure called the amygdala screams out in fear. Other structures may respond with delight, and in this case they fire off dopamine, in my opinion the most potent of all the pleasure transmitters.

Dopamine is just one of the four big feel-good chemicals your brain produces. Exercise junkies will regale you with stories of the endorphin high they get after doing a gruelling triathlon. New mothers often describe feeling very calm when breastfeeding due to their brain producing oxytocin, so they are relaxed and the milk flows more easily. Serotonin is the other big one, and is produced in the brain and digestive system. My metaphor goes like this: if endorphins are like having a single vodka and cranberry juice, serotonin is a double vodka and Red Bull, and dopamine, the gruntiest of them all, is like a dry martini, stirred, not shaken, no ice, no olives, drunk while listening to crooner Dean Martin.

2. Cerebral cortex

The cerebral cortex is the most important part of our brain (at least in the field of psychology) because it is what makes us human. It is the most

DOPAMINE, SHAKEN, NOT STIRRED.

highly developed part of the human brain and is responsible for thinking, perceiving, and producing and understanding language. Most information processing occurs in the cerebral cortex. Let's call it the *rational* part of the brain.

So back to that question about losing control. This quote from neuroscientist Joseph LeDoux sums it up in a nutshell (my preferred form of explanation):

'Connections from the emotional systems to the cognitive systems are stronger than connections from the cognitive systems to the emotional systems.'

Some theorists refer to this as the 'amygdala hijack'. The message and sensations coming from the deeper part of the brain are so powerful they bombard their way through the cerebral cortex like a wrecking ball through a pair of fishnet stockings.

Another thing people ask me is, 'How come when I try to get rid of these worrisome thoughts, they just won't go away?'

Have you ever noticed that the harder you try to stop thinking about something, the harder it is to stop? It seems that the more effort you put into avoiding that thought, the more it just keeps popping up.

Let's do a little exercise:

Now, while I have your attention, I *don't* want you to think about camels. I don't want you to visualise camels or deserts. No cushion covers decorated with camels. No pictures from the front cover of *National Geographic*. I want you stay focused and not think about camels.

How's it going? Plenty of camels, I bet.

Psychologist Daniel Wegner describes it this way:

The funny thing is that when you're trying not to think about things, you have to remember what it is you aren't thinking about. Hence the memory—the part of the mind that is trying to keep the thought fresh—in a paradoxical way is going to then activate the thought.

I like to imagine it this way. Your cerebral cortex is very busy and official, trying to get rid of the troublesome camel thoughts. It is under direct instructions to cease any thinking to do with said animals. Then the memory wakes up from a bit of a snooze, having heard all this commotion about not thinking about something.

Then all of a sudden you're thinking about camels again.

It's quite a mystery how this happens, but then the brain still holds many mysteries. What I am clear about, though, is that there is no point telling a worrier to 'just stop worrying'. It's about as useful as telling you to stop thinking about camels. (There they are again!)

BEHAVIOUR

Worrisome overthinking is described as a 'cognitive behaviour'. It is classified as a behaviour because it is something that we *do*. It's not only an internal thought process, it also has a whole behavioural repertoire. It involves bodily gestures like pacing, sighing, rubbing the furrowed brow—almost as

though it's a ritualised dance.

Some theorists have suggested that these behaviours, which serve no apparent purpose, can be a form of distraction in the moment to calm yourself down. The consensus of psychologists is that they are a person's body signalling to them that they are overwhelmed.

Whatever the specific purpose of the activity, what is unquestionably evident is that these behaviours occur. So there you have it: worrisome overthinking is defined as a behaviour, even though it is a thought process.

As I mentioned earlier, if you are a chronic worrisome overthinker or worrier then there is a 25 to 40 per cent chance that one or more of your children could be genetically predisposed to worry, just like you possibly were. (Just to revisit that earlier definition of worry, it is 'the prediction of negative catastrophic outcomes'.)

As with almost everything, 'nature' and 'nurture' work together (this is called epigenetics). Hence, children learn about how to manage—or not manage—life's challenges through watching their parents, just as you would have.

WHAT GROWN-UPS DO !

It's called role-modelling. Children only know they are safe when the adults around them are OK. So every furrowed brow, every time your hand clutches your face, they've got their eyes peeled, because that is how they survive.

They hear all the gasping and sighing; they see the tears, the shoulders rounded down, the pacing. Not only do they see all of this gesturing, they also notice that the people around them start to behave differently.

Dad might say things like, 'Now you kids be quiet and leave your mother alone, she's got a lot on her mind.'

Other adults may appear, making cups of tea or pouring wine and generally being consoling. With all of this activity going on, in a child's mind this is a very important behaviour and one to take very seriously.

Some people with a tendency to worry may spend time sitting alone, drinking, unapproachable and grumpy. You may have experienced the 'silent treatment' (AKA sulking) in your childhood. Never being told what the problem was and whether or not you were the reason for it may have caused distress.

Hence, when they witness the behaviour of worry, children start to believe that to worry is important. If it's what the grown-ups do, it must be really important and vital to adult survival.

Often parents who worry excessively have a tendency to be very over-protective of their children (AKA helicopter parenting). This inadvertently gives the child the message that the world is a dangerous place full of potential disasters, and that in order to be safe you always need to be super-aware. This promotes fear-based hypervigilance.

I'm not meaning to be a scaremonger and give you something else to overthink! But with the understanding we now have of the genetic predisposition to anxiety, it is better for you to be aware of this information than not. 'Forewarned is forearmed', as they say.

The other good news is that there are excellent books available for children on how they can manage their fears and tackle the 'Worry Monster'. I can recommend *Wilma Jean the Worry Machine* by Julia Cook, *What To Do When You Worry Too Much* by Dawn Huebner, and *Is a Worry Worrying You?* by Ferida Wolff and Harriet May Savitz.

EMOTIONS AND MOOD

As you can see, our behaviour and biology are indivisibly linked. Remember the diagram opposite? What we do affects our physical being, and our biological state impacts on our behaviour, our thinking and our emotions.

Within this sphere, the most common feelings associated with overthinking are:

- excessive anxiety—unease, tension, stress, fretfulness
- feeling wound-up or restless
- irritability
- lowered mood—feeling flat, uninterested
- emotional distress/fear.

With endless overthinking the brain becomes hypervigilant, constantly on the lookout for anything it perceives to be dangerous or worrisome. This creates a state of living in fear and agitation, with all the accompanying biological responses we explored earlier (e.g. overproduction of adrenaline and cortisol). Therefore, it stands to reason that how you feel emotionally is going to be profoundly

influenced by all the other factors we have been discussing.

Let me link them up for you:

You're not sleeping well, because you wake throughout the night ruminating and worrying—maybe about problems at work, financial concerns or the health of your children.

Even if you do manage to get back to sleep, you wake up not feeling refreshed from the little sleep you did manage to get.

Tired, fatigued and anxious, you feel less tolerant of events in your day-to-day life, such as the family at breakfast, getting the kids ready for school, and the traffic. With less tolerance, you are likely to feel irritable and snappy.

Your sense of joy begins to fade. You become increasingly uninterested in the things you used to love doing: listening to music, cooking, gardening, walking. You may find that your overall enjoyment levels are down and spending time with others becomes a chore rather than a pleasure. This lessening of the ability to enjoy your usual activities (anhedonia) is considered to have biological foundations and is a symptom of depression.

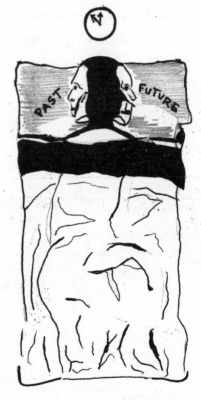

TOO TIRED TO SLEEP

Before we leave this section on the impact of worrisome overthinking on our emotional state, I would like to mention that it is very clear in all the research that it has long-term effects on mood, and one very strong connection is with depression.

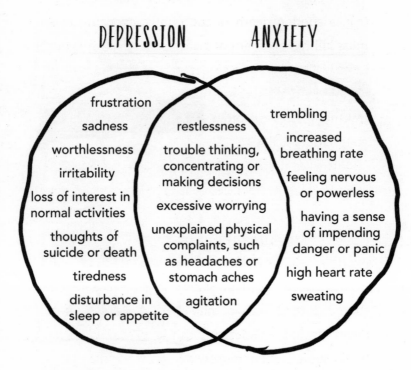

DEPRESSION   ANXIETY

frustration

sadness

worthlessness

irritability

loss of interest in
normal activities

thoughts of
suicide or death

tiredness

disturbance in
sleep or appetite

restlessness

trouble thinking,
concentrating or
making decisions

excessive worrying

unexplained physical
complaints, such
as headaches or
stomach aches

agitation

trembling

increased
breathing rate

feeling nervous
or powerless

having a sense
of impending
danger or panic

high heart rate

sweating

As you can see in the interlocking diagram opposite, depression, anxiety and excessive worrying are inextricably linked. I like to use the metaphor of a car battery to explain this phenomenon.

Think of your inner source of energy (biology) as the car battery. You leave your headlights on. This would be synonymous with a major disaster (e.g. a sudden death in the family, exposure to a mass killing, or a natural disaster that destroys your home). The response to something of this nature would be more likely to fit into the category of post-traumatic stress disorder (PTSD). Within an hour, your battery is flat.

But what if you just leave your parking lights or inside lights on? It will take much, much longer, but your battery still eventually goes flat.

So, with ongoing anxiety and worrisome overthinking grumbling away, your battery will eventually go flat (depression)—it just takes longer than it would with a major event. People often decide to just 'soldier on', thinking they will feel better soon. But our battery doesn't work like that.

Hence, I would like to emphasise the importance of not ignoring these warning signs. When you start to experience your battery going flat—*pay attention*. Your body is telling you something. Don't forget the old adage: if you can 'nip things in the bud', they tend to not get worse.

COGNITION

We have spoken about how biology impacts on behaviour and emotions, how behaviour impacts on biology, and how emotions impact on behaviour. However, the most important sphere in my opinion is that of cognition. I refer to it as the 'headquarters'. The cognitive sphere refers to conscious mental activities: thinking, understanding, learning and remembering.

Let me provide you with a cognitive-behavioural illustration to make my point. If you hold a pen in your hand, and hold your hand steady, both your hand and the pen will remain in the same position (that is, unless you have a movement disorder). When your brain sends a message to your hand to move to the left, that will happen—but not without the thought commanding the behaviour.

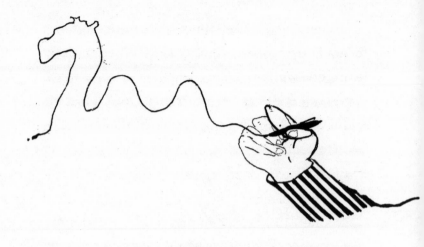

This illustrates how the thinking (cognition) is ultimately in control. Hence, the headquarters. For the most part our cognitive processing rules the roost (the startle response being the exception—for example, if you touch something hot your hand will move away without you having to think about it).

The same applies to the other spheres. For example, if you are overthinking something and worrying about the future and everything going terribly wrong, you will switch on anxiety (biology) and fear (emotion).

Another aspect of this inter-connectedness between the spheres that I believe is essential to understand is that the thought-processing of your brain is in fact a biological phenomenon. By this I mean that the brain is just another organ of your body. Our emotions are a manifestation of a sophisticated mood-regulation system. It is all nature and science.

So often in the contemporary First World, we speak of emotions and intelligence in very abstract and often romantic ways. People often say things like, 'That little Stephanie is so gifted on the piano.' A gift from who and where? I think to myself. (I suspect DNA, in some miraculous way.)

Biology, cognition and suicide

There is also a link between biology and cognition when discussing suicide and depression. I believe it is not part of Mother Nature's evolutional brief for the organism (us) to commit suicide. Animals will fight for their lives. In extreme conditions, we will drink urine and eat human flesh to survive. So in my mind, suicide as a result of severe depression is a disease process.

As someone who carries a diagnosis of bipolar illness, I personally experience this disease process in a very debilitating way. When I am manic or profoundly depressed, I recognise that it is an illness process.

When people get sick with a depressive illness, they sometimes start to contemplate suicide. As they become more unwell, they may begin to think about how they will kill themselves. This to me is not natural. It occurs when a biological process begins to impact on the brain and its cognition in a severely negative way.

This is a very depressing subject, as I know that suicide can occur for a number of different reasons (e.g. chronic anxiety, impulsivity and substance abuse). These also provide very powerful examples of the links between biology and cognition.

In summary, the brain and its cognition dictate behaviour and emotions, and impact significantly on biology. These factors are without doubt entwined.

Now, let's get back to the specific cognitive processing that is troubling you . . .

CHAPTER FOUR

WORRISOME OVERTHINKING (AKA WORRY)

I n my clinical practice I work with an average of seven people a day. Six of those present with anxiety, and four out of those six present with worrisome overthinking.

In the course of getting to know these people I always ask if they overthink or worry. Older people tend to say worry, and the younger ones—25 and under—say overthink. However, when I enquire as to the nature of their overthinking, they describe the same content as the self-confessed worriers, i.e. predicting negative catastrophic outcomes.

So, from now on I am going to refer to worrisome overthinking as 'worry'. It takes less time to type, and in my opinion refers to the same cognitive process.

WORRY, BELIEFS, MYTHS AND ANECDOTES

Many people that I work with know that this type of thinking is causing them health problems, sleep disturbance and fatigue. However, despite this, many are still reluctant to give away the practice (habit), as they believe that it keeps them safe. That it keeps them motivated and prevents bad things happening. That if they stop worrying something bad will certainly happen.

This is mythology and superstition.

Let me highlight this absurdity for you. Imagine that you and I are sitting in my office and I ask you, 'How are you?' You reach out to find the nearest object that could be wood, then tap yourself on the head and say, 'Good—touch wood.'

Now imagine an alien sitting in the room and watching that.

How would it look? Ridiculous, I would imagine. The alien must be thinking, *WTF has tapping yourself on the head after touching a piece of furniture or an unsuspecting window frame got to do with how these humans feel?*

Got the picture? It is simply a weird, superstitious behaviour like throwing salt about, or avoiding walking under ladders, or opening umbrellas inside.

I hate to tell you this, but worry is exactly the same. It is a superstitious behaviour that then becomes a habit.

Let me illustrate for you:

Imagine a mother of two daughters in their late teens. The girls are going to a party and travelling in a car with boys, one of whom is the designated driver. Oh, and I forgot to mention there will be alcohol.

Late in the evening, Mother starts to pace, back and forth, back and forth, constantly looking out the window. Father, watching sport on television, says, 'Come and relax. Let them go and have fun— they're at that age.'

Mother looks towards him in disgust and replies: 'It's all very well for you watching the television. I'm just letting you know that someone in this house has to worry. God knows what would happen if I didn't worry—the whole family would fall apart. It's not that I want to do the worrying, but given that you refuse to worry, I have to!'

Then, as happenstance would have it, the teenagers are involved in a minor car accident, not of their own making. But they do end up at the local hospital with minor injuries. In this moment in time the worry and the incident collide.

In response to this coincidence, the mother receives further evidence (perceptually speaking)

that there *is, was, and always will be* a need to worry! Mother now continues to believe that there was a need to worry about her children in case something bad happened. She now also believes that if she had worried more, and was not distracted by her TV-watching husband, she could have prevented the accident.

This example illustrates well how worry is maintained, as well as the belief in its necessity.

So here you have it, two of the major beliefs involved in the superstition of worry:
1. the preventative power of worry, and
2. the predictive power of worry.

The reality is that worry is a cognitive (thought) process, and the last time I looked, thinking cannot move or change matter. Nor can it control what occurs in the world.

You could be planning an outdoor wedding and

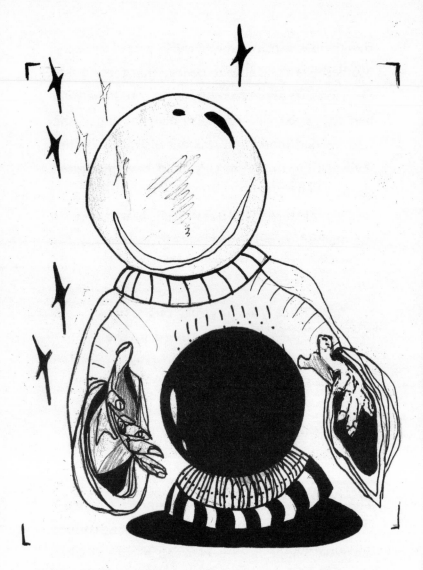

THE PREDICTIVE POWER OF WORRY

you immediately start worrying about it raining. But no matter how much you worry, you will not be able to control the weather. What you can do, however, is take action and put up a marquee.

> The bottom line is, you will gain nothing by worrying— apart from ulcers and irritable bowel syndrome, to name but a few physical side-effects.

I have a tendency to make a point over and over if it's important, and these are concepts that I really want you to get! Without further ado, let me give you another example of the total redundancy of worry.

DOES WORRY WORK?

This point here is to once again highlight the futility of worry—because until you believe this, you will remain reluctant to let it go.

In your mind's eye, I want you to imagine that

you and I are in my office. It has wooden window frames, a little filing cabinet and two comfy chairs. We each have a glass of water.

I am your therapist, and am sitting just across from you, next to the little cabinet. I ask you to stare at my glass of water and imagine it is full of red wine. Also, imagine that I have a habit of opening and closing the cabinet drawers and at the same time throwing my legs and feet about—at all times compromising the stability of the imaginary glass of red wine.

As I sit, pretending to worry about what could happen (predicting), I stare at the glass and hope and pray that the glass does not fall. In anticipation of such disaster, my thinking could look like this:

OMG what if that drink falls onto the carpet, and then what if the stain won't come out, and then what if the carpet can't be replaced, and the insurance can't pay for it, and I can't pay for it, and then I end up with no job and homeless?

Down the spiral of negative thinking I go. It's a bit like flushing myself down a toilet—and I may as well do that, for all the good it does.

Back in the office, I could, of course, sit for a long time freaking out about the possibility of the glass falling and ruining the carpet, resulting in my getting evicted and eventually in the destruction of my life as I know it. *Or* I could move the glass away from the edge and minimise the 'probability' of the glass tipping over.

So, we can see from this example that while **behaviour changes the outcome**, the worrisome **thinking changes nothing**. The probability of the imagined negative event occurring is reduced by **action not thought**.

PROBABILITY OVERESTIMATION

Have a look at the chart on the next page. As you will see, when it all comes down to it, only the tiniest amount of what you spend your precious time ruminating and worrying about ever actually happens.

A table of worry

40% of all things we worry about never happen
30% have already happened and we can't do anything about them
12% needless worries about health
10% petty miscellaneous issues
8% real worries (½ we can do little about, the other ½ we can)

One of the unique aspects of the worrier's cognition is the constant overestimation of catastrophically bad things happening. Not only is your anxiety elevated by how much you overestimate the likelihood of negative events occurring in your life, but there is also often the added belief that you will be unable to cope when these events do occur.

When you look closer at these facts, it becomes more and more evident that you are spending a considerable amount of your waking hours frightening yourself. You are suffering more as a result of your imagination than reality.

'WHAT IF?'—THE WORRY MANTRA

'What if . . . ?' Those two seemingly innocent words in combination form the question responsible for triggering the bulk of worrisome overthinking. Recognise the following thoughts?

- Yeah, but what if that happens?
- What if they do that?
- What if I do that and then that happens?
- What if I can't cope?

The 'What if' mantra can keep you meditating on possible drama for hours at a time, taking your thinking round and round in an endless spiral of negative prediction.

Each time you kick off another spiral of worry, you are continuously switching on your fight/flight mechanism, producing adrenaline and eventually exhausting your system. This is also the type of thinking that will wake you up in the night, leaving you feeling unrefreshed in the morning.

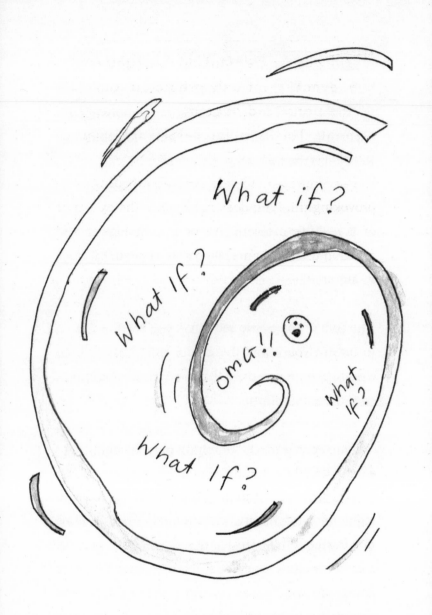

> In worrisome thinking, a negative event is not only predicted, but the perceived outcome is invariably huge. This is called **catastrophising**.

It is also important to note that this form of anxiety-provoking thinking does not require the existence of a real-life problem. All of this biological and emotional disturbance is being created by your thoughts. The trigger is not *external*, it is *internal*.

The goal of the above section of the book has been to inform you about the complexity of worrisome overthinking—not only the mechanics of biology, emotions, behaviour and cognition, but also the complex nature of worry itself.

As a cognitive habit, it is a slippery phenomenon, a bit like Pythonissa, the slippery soothsayer.

Worrisome overthinking slips and slides through logic and rationality, determined to exist—and making it often very resistant to treatment. I observe this in my clinic when I ask a client, 'So how's it all going—do you feel as though you have overcome your worrisome overthinking?'

Pythonissa, the slippery soothsayer.

They reply, 'Yep, I only worry about important things these days.'

Oh dear.

You see, saying that they will save worrying for the bigger problems clearly infers that worry still has value and can still change reality. My clients often believe that they are 'cured' because they have decided that they won't 'sweat the small stuff' and they now save their worrying for the important things in life.

Not true. Worry is worry is worry.

Worry continues to be maintained by superstitious belief systems and the mythology that reinforces its existence, momentum and influence. The therapeutic task is to challenge the beliefs associated with worry, utilising factually based evidence.

PART 2

OVER-COMING OVER-THINKING

CHAPTER FIVE

WHAT TO DO ABOUT OVERTHINKING: THE THERAPEUTIC MODEL

IT'S JUST YOU, ME AND THE WHITEBOARD.

Welcome to my office. It's just you, me and the whiteboard. Our weekly sessions are about to begin (be prepared for homework!).

You have already filled out a bit of paperwork for me, so I can formulate my treatment plan based on the information you have provided. You describe the following experiences:

Biology

- abdominal and bowel problems
- restless, non-refreshing sleep
- heart palpitations
- shallow breathing
- fatigue
- anxiety

Emotions (Mood)

- irritable
- frustrated
- despondent

- sense of sadness
- fearful

Behaviour
- avoidance
- withdrawal
- excessive worrying

Cognition (Mind)
- pessimistic
- self-critical
- difficulty making decisions
- poor concentration

You've hit the jackpot. You are now a diagnosed worrisome overthinker!

Up on the whiteboard goes the CBT model—the perfect vehicle for mapping out your troublesome experiences (symptoms).

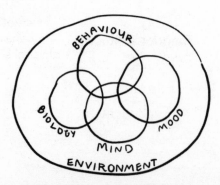

The next step is to illustrate for you how the model translates into a practical, working application.

It works like this:

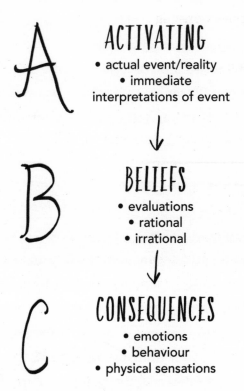

A **ACTIVATING**
- actual event/reality
- immediate interpretations of event

↓

B **BELIEFS**
- evaluations
- rational
- irrational

↓

C **CONSEQUENCES**
- emotions
- behaviour
- physical sensations

A = REALITY, AN ACTUAL EVENT, THE TRIGGER

'A' is never defined as the problem. As I always say: 'It's reality and shit happens!'

As I mentioned to you earlier, when it comes to worry, the trigger can be external and/or internal. For example, a phone call bringing bad news would be considered an **external trigger**.

If you are sitting on the couch at home and start to think 'what if?', sending you on a downward spiral, your thinking acts as a trigger. This is referred to as an **internal trigger**.

B = YOUR COGNITION/THINKING

The thinking included in this section is both rational and irrational, incorporating beliefs, perceptions and evaluations.

You see, in cognitive theory it is not simply a matter of *what* you are thinking, we're interested in the *how* of your thinking. In other words, we're examining the meaning that you are inferring from the 'A' (the trigger/event).

In the cognitive therapy world, *inference* means

what you read into something, what you assume about it. For example, 'What does this say about me? What does this mean to me?'

Let's say you and I read exactly the same book. I find it exhilarating and enlightening—close to the best book I have ever read.

You, meanwhile, have forced yourself to get to the last page—and have only done so because it is required reading for this month's book club—and you declare it the most boring book you have ever come across.

Hard to believe it is exactly the same book! But this illustrates very clearly how different perceptual filters, and the different ways we process information, can result in opposing opinions and interpretations of events.

This focus on the *how* of your thinking (i.e. how you give meaning) is integral in cognitive therapy, and it is in the 'B' section that the therapeutic intervention occurs.

WHAT DOES THIS BOOK SAY ABOUT ME?

Not positive thinking

Importantly, the goal of cognitive therapy is not to teach positive thinking—which I refer to as 'putting sugar on shit!' As a result of cognitive behavioural therapy, your thinking becomes more constructive and helpful, but this is not the same as positive thinking through affirmations.

I mean, think about it: you've been up half the night ruminating and predicting upcoming disasters. You haul yourself out of bed, feeling and looking like a train wreck.

You go to the bathroom, look into the mirror and say to yourself the following, several times over:

- 'I think positive thoughts about myself and others.'
- 'I protect myself against any hurt that comes my way.'
- 'I like the person I see in the mirror.'

How's that going for you?

Don't get me wrong—I'm not against people thinking more positively. But trying to put positive thoughts on top of negative ones is like me telling you, 'Stop thinking about camels.'

Reattribution of meaning

In cognitive theory, meaning is 'reattributed'. By that I mean things are given meaning in a new and different way. By learning how to do this, you learn how to shift irrational fear to a realistic appraisal of the reality, thereby reducing the fear.

For example, you see a mouse in the corner of the room. You panic and leave the room immediately—heart racing, hyperventilating—because in your mind the 'meaning' you have given the mouse goes like this . . .

OMG, a disease-ridden rodent! If I sit down it will come towards me and climb all over me and bite me! I will get the plague and I won't be able to stand it!

Reattributing the meaning would be to structure it more like this . . .

You see the mouse. You don't want it there for hygiene reasons. You tell yourself:

It's more afraid of me, as I am the much bigger creature and it is tiny.

You might get a broom, you might get one of the kids to chase it outside, you may lay a trap—you begin to problem-solve.

By thinking rationally about the mouse—**thinking based in fact**—you are far less likely to have a panic attack and spend the day outside screaming until someone comes home to rescue you.

After reattributing meaning, your thinking is now based in fact and reality. It is now rational and evidence-based—the opposite to the fear-provoking irrational thoughts created in your imagination.

Hence, your thinking becomes more constructive, helpful and, yes, more positive. The difference is that you have given a new meaning to your experience and made it less frightening, rather than merely superimposing the negative with some half-hearted attempt at believing a positive affirmation.

C = YOUR RESPONSES

Biological/emotional/behavioural

Before we go on any further, I need you to *really* pay attention to this equation:

'B' (COGNITION) CREATES THE 'C' (RESPONSES)

As mentioned earlier, the startle response is an exception to this rule, as are what we call 'conditioned emotional responses'. Very briefly, we learned about these responses from Russian doctor Ivan Pavlov and his dogs.

Pavlov found that a dog will salivate as an involuntary response to seeing meat. It will not salivate to an odourless, unappetising bell sound. But pair the bell with the scrummy meat and again the salivation begins.

Hey presto—the response is now conditioned. The dog salivates to the sound of the bell only. Thank you, Pavlov . . .

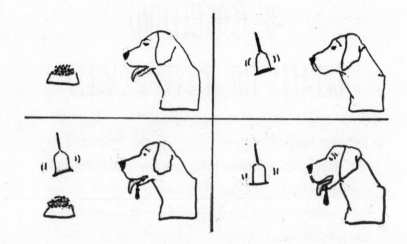

PAVLOV

Let's go back to the rodent, to illustrate the importance of Pavlov's experiments in terms of humans and their anxiety responses. I want to drop in for a minute on my own rodent phobia. (I know this may come as a shock—the first evidence that I am not perfect.)

Imagine a chubby little English girl arriving from 'civilised' England (pre-Brexit) to live in a hydroelectric village in a New Zealand backwater. White skin, covered in mosquito bites, completely inept at negotiating anything other than a footpath, but making a decent effort to fit in.

I join the other kids (but still with my shoes on, bare feet being totally alien to me) running through a small patch of pine trees. The other kids appear to be running gleefully, while for me it is more like a hurried tiptoe through a field of horror. Then the nightmare truly begins. One of the other kids yells out: 'Don't knock that tree!'

I look up and there is the biggest, scariest creature I have ever seen. A tree rat, whose mission in life is to jump on me and kill me with its huge monster teeth. I run screaming, my adrenaline fuelling my fear-driven exit.

Fear develops into phobias because of memory.

Over the years my fear generalised across all rodents, no matter how big or small. Bats were a particular nightmare, as they are rats that fly! No one was going to convince me they were just cute little furry things—fact or not!

So, just like Pavlov's dogs, I became conditioned. Anything remotely rodent-like activated that same fear, as if I was back in that pine forest with that giant, life-threatening rat. This is an 'emotional memory', like the child and the dog earlier.

Humans remember via all of their senses:

- Sound: Oh, I remember that tune so clearly, that was the night I lost my virginity.
- Smell: Mmm, every time I smell that soup it reminds me of summer at the beach house with Granny.
- Touch: I love the feel of sand between my toes, it takes me back to walking along the beach with my first girlfriend (who subsequently dumped me).
- Taste: Salt and vinegar are my absolute favourite potato chips, from as long ago as I can remember.

EMOTIONAL MEMORY

The sensory memory that is often overlooked is the emotional memory: the vivid recall of feelings. Emotional memory may not evoke feelings that are as intense as those experienced at the time of the event, but the feelings still can cause great joy or pain.

The emotions that are linked to memory are messaged from the amygdala. Once these emotional memories are activated, they will catapult the experience from the past into the present. (Remember the wrecking ball from page 54.)

When the emotional memory is triggered, if it is based on something frightening it can result in significant distress. I am going to show you how to measure this distress as part of your homework (see the next chapter) in just a moment.

CHAPTER SIX

STARTING THE THERAPY

A THE 'A' IS REALITY, IT IS <u>NOT</u> THE PROBLEM.

↓

C THE 'C' IS WHERE THE PROBLEMS EXIST. PEOPLE COME TO THERAPY BECAUSE THEY ARE FEELING BAD AND ARE NOT HAPPY ABOUT HOW THEY ARE BEHAVING.

↓

B THE 'B'—THE COGNITION— IS WHERE THE THERAPEUTIC INTERVENTION OCCURS.

Back to the A-B-C, the working model. In the diagram opposite I have changed the order to A-C-B to help explain further the working dynamics of the therapy.

Nobody wakes up in the morning thinking, I *must go and spend a shitload of money on a psychologist to check whether or not my thinking is factual and evidence-based*. But the fact is, your responses are a reflection of, and are created by, your thinking. Hence, to change how you are feeling you need to change how you are thinking.

The main reason why you don't identify a need to change your thinking is because for the majority of the time, your thinking is providing you with factually based information.

You walk into a room and you see a chair; you know that it is for sitting on.

You approach a red light; you know that means stop. A glass of water is for drinking, etc., etc.

There would appear to be no reason to question your thinking most of the time. However, as I have mentioned to you, your thinking is where the problems are solved.

When your thinking isn't working
for you and is causing you
difficulty in your interpersonal
world, it's therapy time!

By this stage of the book, I would hope that you have gleaned a more in-depth understanding of the workings and importance of cognitive processing, in particular. This knowledge can help you. For this week's homework, we now begin the practical application of the theory.

First we need to collect a bit of what we in the trade call 'baseline data': measuring the starting point and—all going to plan—the point of departure from 'Station Angst'.

The following is a 'Thought Record', sometimes called a 'Thought Diary'. It provides you with a template to describe one or two experiences from your week when you have been distressed as a result of your thinking.

You may find it easier to use your phone to record your thoughts. I really don't mind, as long as I have the information for our next tutorial.

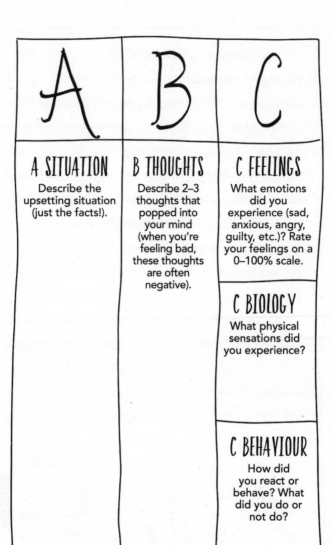

A	B	C
A SITUATION Describe the upsetting situation (just the facts!).	**B THOUGHTS** Describe 2–3 thoughts that popped into your mind (when you're feeling bad, these thoughts are often negative).	**C FEELINGS** What emotions did you experience (sad, anxious, angry, guilty, etc.)? Rate your feelings on a 0–100% scale. **C BIOLOGY** What physical sensations did you experience? **C BEHAVIOUR** How did you react or behave? What did you do or not do?

The Thought Record:
understanding the relationship between
thoughts, feelings and behaviour.

A few tips for your first thought record:

A: Situation. This column is just a factual description of the situation. No feelings, no thoughts—just a description. Keep it nice and concise. Stay focused.

B: Thoughts. These must be automatic, like a stream of consciousness. Rave away and be as negative as you like. Whatever you do, don't censor your thoughts. As you write them down, you may look at them and think, *I can't believe this shit that I am writing down. If Gwendoline sees this, she'll think I'm certifiable.* But the crazier the better as far as I'm concerned! I have to know *how* you are thinking, not how you *think* you should be thinking. If you want this to work, be honest. Remember that if this was real life, you'd be paying a bundle of cash for this therapy!

C: Feelings. You may find it easier to record your emotions first, before your behaviour, as they are what you will experience first.

You will also notice that in this area I have written 'rate your feelings on a 0–100% scale'. These are referred to as SUDS—Subjective Units of Distress. Let me explain: it means that the rating of the distress is a measurement of your personal discomfort.

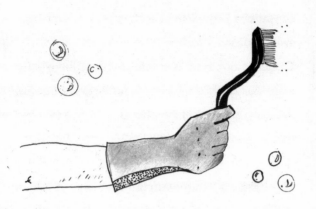

SUDS = SUBJECTIVE UNITS OF DISTRESS

Lots of my clients try to shift their experiences by making comments like, 'I feel so silly being here talking about my little problems. I'm sure you see people with much bigger problems than mine.'

That may be the case, but that is nothing to do with you. If you were going to be fixed by comparing realities, you wouldn't need to be in therapy—you would simply switch on Al Jazeera in the morning, stare at the ravage of another cyclone, another famine, another genocide, and all would be well in your world. No, doesn't work!

C: Biology. This is where you record your physical sensations (e.g. racing heart, shallow breathing, sweaty palms, etc.).

C: Behaviour. Here is where you describe what you were doing while distressed, for instance pacing, avoiding answering the phone, worrying (remember, this is classified as a behaviour).

This baseline information will enable us to measure the changes in your discomfort levels and, of course, to see how you progress.

Don't be concerned
if you don't get it
all sorts of perfect.
It's not a test.

You might find it difficult initially to separate thoughts and feelings. Your description of the event may be a bit wordy. No problem—it doesn't matter. Just one example will be fine.

See you next week for another session.

CHAPTER SEVEN

AN INTRODUCTION TO THOUGHT VIRUSES

Welcome back to my office.

Me: Hi, how's your week been?

You: Not bad. I've written down the things that haven't gone so well.

Me: Excellent. I've had a not-so-bad week. Still working away on *The Book of Overthinking.* But enough of me—back to you. Let me have a look at what you've got there.

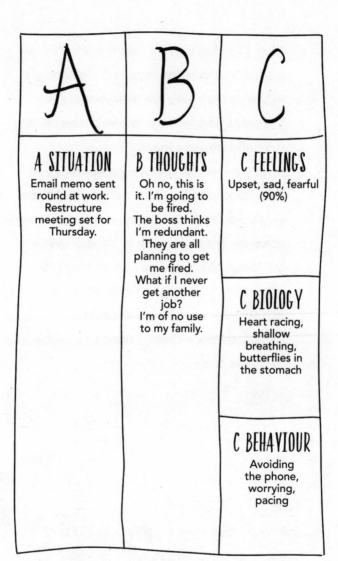

A

A SITUATION

Email memo sent round at work. Restructure meeting set for Thursday.

B

B THOUGHTS

Oh no, this is it. I'm going to be fired.
The boss thinks I'm redundant.
They are all planning to get me fired.
What if I never get another job?
I'm of no use to my family.

C

C FEELINGS

Upset, sad, fearful (90%)

C BIOLOGY

Heart racing, shallow breathing, butterflies in the stomach

C BEHAVIOUR

Avoiding the phone, worrying, pacing

Me: OK, that's an excellent start. You've placed all the responses and the thoughts in the appropriate columns. Separating thoughts and feelings is one of the most difficult things to learn.

Before we go on to analyse what you have recorded, I will introduce you to the cognitive language that you will utilise along the way. These are called 'thought viruses', or thinking errors. They are perceptual filters that you are currently unaware of that distort your perception of reality.

To introduce them, I want to use the 'brain as computer' metaphor.

COMPUTER-MIND ANALOGY

If you think about your brain processing information like a computer, the metaphor would be as follows:

1. You have a hard drive, where all your core beliefs and values are stored from way back when. This includes your early life history, your role-modelling, your value system.

2. Then there is the software package, where your rules of living and your attitudes are stored. These rules often present in your thinking as the 'if/thens'. There you are as a child, learning about how the world and the people in it work. For example, you notice that *if* you behave in a certain way *then* your mother gets very angry. *If* you behave in a different way, *then* your mother appears pleased. In your adult world this could apply to your partner or your boss or a close friend.

3. Then there is the screen. This is where the thoughts you are conscious of in your daily life are displayed.

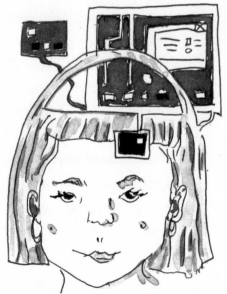

Tricks of the mind—when the brain lies to you

Continuing with the computer metaphor, if you have the equivalent of a virus in the metaphorical processing system, your thoughts become irrational. These irrational thoughts then create exaggerated emotions. However, you believe them to be true. Because, why wouldn't you?

The following is a list of some of these little 'thought viruses' that get into your cognitive processing system and wreak havoc with your interpretation and hence management of your reality. (I will also provide this list as an appendix at the back of the book for easy reference, as you will need to familiarise yourself with them so you can detect them when they are active in your thinking.)

THE THOUGHT VIRUSES

All-or-nothing thinking

The world is seen in very black-and-white terms, using words like: always/never, nobody/everybody, everything/nothing. This is a very rigid way of

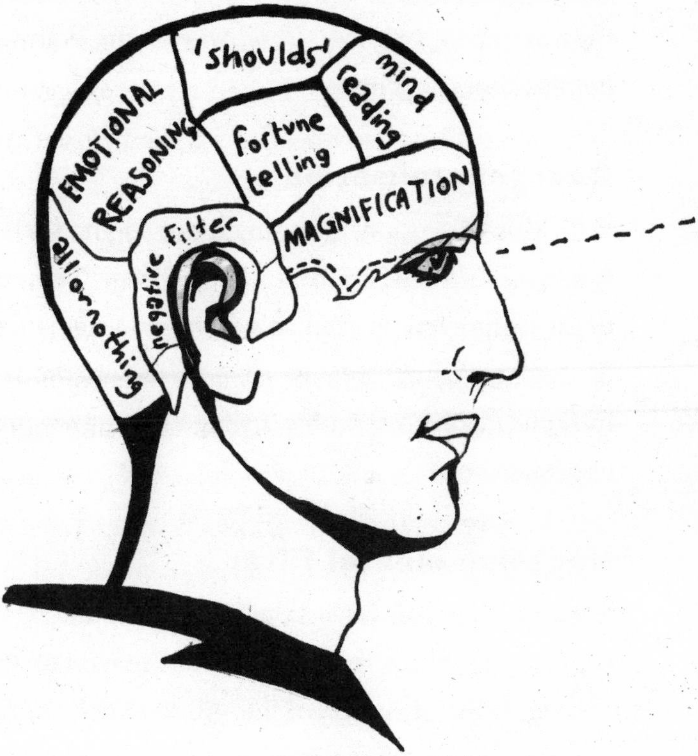

'shoulds'
mind reading
EMOTIONAL REASONING
fortune telling
MAGNIFICATION
filter
negative
all or nothing

thinking, with no room for the 'grey' which makes up all aspects of life. This thinking is in the extreme. You will all know a black-and-white thinker—they are very difficult to have discussions with because they are always right . . . 'my way or the highway' being a popular phrase.

Overgeneralisation

With this distortion, one single not-so-good event is seen as a predictor for a life of misery. This one unpleasant event is seen as a never-ending pattern of defeat. Again, this is an extreme method of interpreting events, with a strong ongoing element of pessimism.

Negative mental filter

Imagine that you have bought a set of filters for your glasses, and whenever you put them on all you can see is the dark side of life. All the positive, fun aspects of your life are filtered out, your only focus being on the negative aspects of any situation.

This filter in particular has a strong relationship with depression and anxiety. Of course, worriers consistently see the world through this lens.

Disqualifying the positive

This thought virus not only focuses on the negative, but also filters out anything positive that you may have achieved. Someone compliments you on a job well done and you reply something along these lines: 'Oh, anyone can do that, it's not that much of a big deal, it was just a stroke of luck.'

This is another way of maintaining a negative belief-set about yourself, your world and your achievements.

Jumping to conclusions

The strongest component of jumping to conclusions is the foundation of assumption. There are no facts to support the thinking and the negative interpretations stem solely from your own beliefs—when, as I have said earlier, *beliefs are not facts*!

There are two elements to this thought virus, both being among the primary contributors to all forms of anxiety:

1. Mind-reading

This is when, based on a whim, you arbitrarily conclude that people are thinking negatively about you, without any evidence that this is true. There are a couple of very spooky elements to this assumption:

- that people are even thinking about you, when the majority of the time they are thinking about themselves.
- that they are thinking exactly the same negative things about you that you are thinking at exactly the same time—now, that has to be some wicked form of black magic!

By now you may be starting to get confused, thinking that other people know what you're thinking when actually you are just thinking about yourself.

The other thing that goes on in this process, called 'projection' (a term coined by the great Sigmund Freud), is that you continue to believe you can read the minds of other people—which of course you cannot—and that other people can read yours—which they cannot. This additional inaccuracy will leave you feeling transparent and vulnerable in your interactions with others.

2. Fortune-telling

Oh, if only this one could be true! But it is not.

Imagine all your problems solved by your being able to predict the Lotto numbers. Yes, the belief in this thought virus is as ridiculous as that.

This is a favourite pastime of the worrisome overthinker—constantly predicting (fortune-telling) negative outcomes.

Chorused with the following:

Yes but, no but, but then, but then what if?

Then it will, and then you will,
and then I will . . .

Then all things will turn to shit forever
just like I told you they would.

'Cos don't you know, baby, I'm a fortune-teller.

So here's the deal: *you're not mind-reading and nor is anybody else.* Nor are you predicting the future, even though the more you worry and bad things do happen, you feel as though you do in fact have this gift. But remember, this is coincidence!

Remember:
Feelings are not facts.
Beliefs are not facts.

Don't be fooled—thought viruses are simply ways that our mind convinces us of something that is not true. We utilise such thoughts to reinforce negative thinking or emotions, such as maintaining feeling sad, anxious and despondent, to name but a few.

Magnification AKA catastrophising

Commonly phrased as: OMG!!!! Bigger than Texas! Massive, huge, colossal, gigantic—when the molehill becomes a mountain. You exaggerate and exaggerate and don't stop exaggerating until you are exhausted from being overwhelmed. It doesn't have to be just your own problems—this filter can be easily applied to everybody else's.

CAT!ASTROPHISING + MAGNIFICATION

This is a good time to remember the definition of worry for our purposes:

'The **prediction** of **negative catastrophic** outcomes.'

↓	↓	↓
fortune-telling	negative filter	catastrophising

You can begin to see how they all play their own little part in f@cking with your head. Let's familiarise you with a few more.

Minimisation

Magnification in reverse. You take the mountains—for example, your significant achievements—and shrink them into molehills. By doing so you get to avoid acknowledging your strengths and desirable qualities, along with diluting any possibility of experiencing anything joyful.

Do yourself a favour, I say. If you still happen to be ruminating when you're six foot under, save the minimising and disqualifying the positive for then.

Emotional reasoning

Less obvious than, say, the fortune-telling and mind-reading distortions, this one is, however, extremely powerful in a subtle and insidious kind of way. Emotional reasoning is convincing yourself that because you feel something it *must* be a fact.

Whenever I arrive at this point I refer to David Burns (a renowned cognitive therapist and author). In his book *Feeling Good: The New Mood Therapy*, he describes exactly what I am trying to convey brilliantly, so there's no need to reinvent the wheel:

Even though your depressing (negative) thoughts may be distorted they nevertheless create a powerful illusion of truth. Let me expose the basis for the deception in blunt terms—your feelings are not facts! In fact your feelings, per se, don't even count—except as a mirror of the way you are thinking. If your perceptions make no sense, the feeling they create will be as absurd as the images reflected in the trick mirrors at an amusement park. But these abnormal emotions feel just as valid and realistic as the genuine feelings created by undistorted thoughts, so you automatically attribute truth to them.

I bet that's got you thinking. If it hasn't, go back and read it again!

Back to emotional reasoning. You get a feeling—fear, despair, sadness—and then you start to believe the irrational thoughts that have created the anxiety, and before you know it you've bought yourself a ticket on the 'Spiralling Worry Ride'.

Time to remember once again:

The **B** (your cognition/thinking) evaluates the **A** (event/reality) then creates the **C** (emotions/behaviour).

'Feelings are a mirror of the way you are thinking.'

—DAVID BURNS

It is essential that you **believe** this, as it is the key to making change.

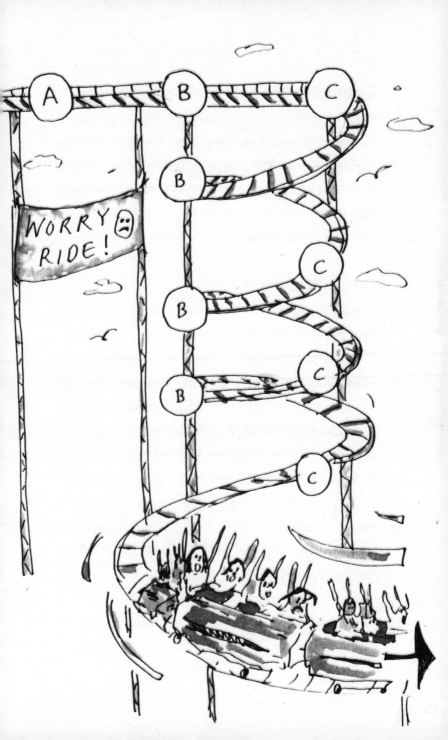

Cognitive reasoning

Very similar to its counterpart virus (emotional reasoning), cognitive reasoning is based on the assumption that because you think and even perhaps *believe* something to be true, then it must be so.

Once again, unless based in fact *this is not true either*.

To illustrate:

You remain seated and I stand up in front of you and ask, 'Is the world flat?'

For a brief moment, you think, *Time to change therapists—this woman is losing touch with reality.* Then you adamantly reply, 'No. It's round, of course.'

Standing defiantly, I look down at my feet and say, 'Well, it feels flat to me.' (emotional reasoning) 'It looks flat and I'm standing up straight. How could I possibly be standing here like this if it was round? I believe it is flat.' (cognitive reasoning)

You, now slightly tired of this masquerade, bluntly reply, 'The fact is the world is round—there is scientific evidence and proof.'

Therein lies the point: *there is evidence.*

To believe anything else is cognitive reasoning.

I'll say it again: beliefs are not facts.

Biological reasoning

As far as I know, I have made this one up.

By now you should have an understanding of both cognitive and emotional reasoning. I have decided there was another element to this idea of convincing yourself that something must be true when it is not.

Physical sensations are often the first things we become aware of at times of distress. You remember the story about the bump in the gum (see page 32), and how such discoveries magnify for the individual with health anxiety? However, this phenomenon can also exist without that diagnosis.

For instance, you haven't been sleeping and you're feeling exhausted and constantly anxious. Then your gut starts to play up. You then start to negatively overthink what might be happening. Round and round you go, back into the worry spiral, arriving at a self-diagnosis (with the assistance of Dr Google) of—on a good day—appendicitis, and on a not-so-good day bowel cancer. You have arrived at this point by interpreting a signal from your biology, giving it a meaning and panicking without any facts.

The A-B-C depiction would look like this:

A (event) -> **B** (thoughts/meaning-giving) -> **C** (responses: emotions/biology/behaviour)

A: SITUATION
Stomach ache

B: THOUGHTS
OMG what's that pain?

This is the worst pain I have ever experienced!!

I can't stand this! I'm not going to make it through.

What if?? What if??? What if??? Bowel cancer

C: FEELINGS
fear, anxiety, distress

C: BIOLOGY
racing heart, shallow breathing, sweaty, more stomach pain

C: BEHAVIOUR

worrying, keep Googling, pacing

So there you have it, biological reasoning in action.

Neurogastroenterology— the two brains

I'm just going to introduce you to another vital piece of information about the gut, which adds to the above scenario.

We place so much emphasis on how we feel internally that people talk about their 'gut feelings' and make decisions based upon them. Yes, we do experience 'gut feelings', but given that 95 per cent of our serotonin receptors reside in the gut it's hardly surprising.

This is where neuroscience once again gets really fascinating—so as you appear interested, here's another little hors-d'oeuvre from neurobiology. I bet you didn't know that we have brain cells in the digestive tract (AKA the enteric nervous system). These neurons are referred to as the second brain, additional to the brain at the top of the spinal cord.

New research now suggests that these neurons may actually be the very first 'brain' that our mammalian ancestors evolved.

The connection between the two brains lies at the heart of many afflictions, both physical and psychiatric e.g. anxiety, depression, ulcers, irritable bowel syndrome. Research also shows that the majority of individuals with anxiety and depression will also have disturbance in their gastrointestinal system.
—Dr Emeran Mayer, *The Mind–Gut Connection*

Hence when I go on about how worrisome overthinking creates anxiety, and anxiety impacts adversely on your health and in particular the gastrointestinal system—such as irritable bowel syndrome—I'm not joking.

If you're interested in the research on the 'second brain' it's well worth reading the article 'A brain in the head, and one in the gut' by Harriet Brown in *The New York Times*, August 2005 (Google it).

Personalisation

This thought virus can on its own create a lot of emotional pain, for it is the belief that you are the cause of external events that you have nothing to do with, or that you were not primarily responsible for. As a result you can end up feeling exposed, vulnerable and guilty, and respond by becoming withdrawn and avoidant. If you start to blame yourself for the external events, you will feel angry and powerless.

Once again this distortion, although creating distress and vulnerability, also involves a significant degree of narcissism, because it is based on the belief that everything that goes on around you is somehow attached to you.

Text messaging is a classic example of how personalisation occurs. You text your partner early afternoon, casually expecting a reply straight away—well, within reason.

Thirty minutes later, still nothing.

Time to check the phone, make sure it's switched on, check that the ring tone isn't on silent. You switch the phone off in case it needs a reboot, because the entire network may have gone down since you sent your text. Then you start repeat texting.

Hi just me, did you get my last text?

Hi it's me again, nothing major just thought I would have heard.

Everything ok?

Look, I'm really sorry about what I said last night. I meant it as a joke, but I can see how it could have been taken the wrong way. Love you xxxx

Do you ever intend to answer this f@cking phone?

Ok have it your way!! F@ck you if you can't take a joke!! I'm moving out!!!!!

Hi honey, just got your txt, been in an emergency board meeting. What's up?

Look familiar? Thought so! Can you see the thinking process going around and around in your head like an unwanted tune? Can you hear yourself 'overthinking'?

Here's the script for that thinking, in case you've forgotten (or misplaced the thoughts alongside the camels).

CAMEL-mojis!

Here we go—experience that downward circular movement as your thoughts take you down that spiral, straight into that metaphorical toilet . . .

Mmmmm . . . still haven't heard. Even when she's busy she'll usually make the time to touch base. Won't hurt to send another text now it's been 10 minutes.

*I'll wait a while until I send another one, otherwise she'll start thinking (**mind-reading**) that I'm trying to be manipulative, and then she won't come home (**fortune-telling, negative mental filter**).*

*F@ck it!!! If she wants to play this game (**cognitive and emotional reasoning**) I'm not taking this shit!! (**catastrophising . . . still personalising**)*

*It's not like I haven't apologised, but still no response. She thinks she can treat me like an idiot. (**more mind-reading, negative filter, cognitive and emotional reasoning**)*

I can't take this!!!

This last thought takes us to the next thought virus.

I can't stand it!!!!

This is the perfect thought command to strip you of any remaining tolerance. As soon as you start telling yourself that you literally cannot stand another minute, another word, another day, you will start to believe it to be true!

Once this thought process begins, your resilience crumbles. In this very overwhelming moment (don't forget that you have imagined it is that!), you either break down in tears or rise up with anger—neither of which are remotely necessary or factually engineered.

When you convince yourself that you 'can't stand' something, you are also telling yourself that you can't take on new situations, because they will be too stressful. For example:

I can't talk to those strangers at the party, because they will think I'm boring, and then I won't know what to say, and then I'll look silly. I just can't do it, I can't stand it.

Looks like a lot of jumping to conclusions and 'I can't stand its', to me.

The obstacle that you are telling yourself you have to get through is *only in your mind*. There is *no physical obstacle* to you going over there and striking up a conversation. The obstacle is a cognitive distortion.

Look back on the worst situation you have ever been through in your life. You may have lost a parent, had a nasty divorce, lost your job.

You are still here, so I'm guessing you got through it OK. It would appear that thinking based in truth would go more like this: *This isn't great, but I've been through worse and made it to the other side.*

Stick with the facts, ladies and gentlemen.

The obstacle that you are telling yourself you have to get through is only in your mind.

Labelling

Just briefly, as we haven't got much time left in our session today and this is a lot of knowledge to take on board . . . labelling has the same essence as overgeneralising, but as well as picking out what you did wrong, you spring into: *I always make this same mistake, I'm such a f@ckwit!*

You can, of course, project this thinking onto others: *He never gets it right. May as well do it myself! Idiot.*

These are clearly very emotionally laden neuro-linguistics (the language of thought), with the potential to create a war within your own head.

Shoulds, musts and have tos

This section of knowledge is so crucial to you that I'm going to save it for our next tutorial. Take a break—see you next week.

CHAPTER EIGHT

THE SHOULDS, MUSTS AND HAVE TOS

Me: Anything to report—good, bad or otherwise?

You: I over-reacted to a text situation and now I'm sleeping on a couch at my parents' place. When does this cognitive stuff start to work? I thought it was supposed to help me manage my feelings?

Me: Well, we have only met a couple of times, and learning about cognitive therapy is like learning a new language—the only difference being it is centred on the language of thought. Hang in, we're nearly there.

As I explained in our last session, the 'should, must and have to' thought virus requires a bit of attention. I spent a lot of time on these distortions in my last book, *The Book of Knowing*. I would like to take this opportunity to plagiarise my own work and repeat some of those ideas here.

First of all, the words 'should', 'must' and 'have to' all mean the same, and hence create the same emotional, biological and behavioural responses.

The table below shows how destructive the 'should' statements can be—particularly with how you feel about yourself, other people and the world.

Thoughts	Effects
I should have	guilt / regret
I shouldn't have	guilt / self-loathing
They should have	anger / frustration / disappointment
They shouldn't have	resentment / anger / frustration
I have to	pressure / tension / obligation
I must	more pressure / more tension

Now there's a bucket full of fun! (Not!) Look at all of those hideous emotions, biological tension and distress. It's amazing that we still believe in this word and give it such a predominant place in our thinking.

I am very passionate and adamant about my opinions of the word 'should'. It's a control-based word, just like 'must' and 'have to'. Certain orthodox religions have used such words over the centuries (remember 'thou shalt'/'thou shalt not'?) to govern their followers through control and guilt.

I have been challenged over the years on this, with people saying that if we removed the control words from our thinking and belief systems there would be anarchy. I remember one guy I was working with, a controlled negative perfectionist. He was horrified when I suggested that he eliminate the words 'should', 'must' and 'have to' from his thinking vocabulary. He was fearful that he would become demotivated and hence fail. Lots of people fear this loss of motivation.

However, fear-driven motivation makes people ill. True motivation comes from the desire to do something.

This brings us to the two classifications used in cognitive theory when discussing the word 'should':

Instructional 'shoulds'

These are what are used to teach children. For example, children 'should' be taught never to put a fork into an electrical socket. Teaching that hopefully minimises the risk of the child getting electrocuted. So it is a *helpful* should.

Instructional 'shoulds' are also used when providing instructions, say for the use of a computer or some piece of machinery. For example, 'You must always switch this on before you activate the software, or the computer will crash.' Again, this is helpful and factually based information.

Instructional 'shoulds' are helpful.

Moralistic shoulds

Here is where the problems occur. For example, 'You should do it my way because my way is the right way.' 'You shouldn't believe in that God because my God is the right one.' 'You shouldn't be driving that car, it's sooo . . . not cool.'

> Moralistic 'shoulds' are based on values, beliefs and expectations. **Question:** Whose beliefs are the right ones? **Answer:** None of them. Beliefs are not facts.

Try to be very aware of the 'shoulds, musts and have tos'. They create pressure, and pressure can cause illness.

When they take the form of expectations, shoulds also create problems in your relationships. The assumption is that people should do and think what you do. No surprise—they don't.

Here's an example:

Imagine that I'm your neighbour. (If that thought is a bit too much, rustle up a camel.)

Anyway, I come over and ask to borrow the brand-new lawn mower I noticed you bought last week.

You: (nervously) Sure, but please be careful—it's just new.

Me: No problem—cheers.

Nearly a week passes before I bring the mower back. You've seen it left out in the rain a few times, but you want to avoid conflict so you say nothing.

But during that entire week you can't help but think, *She shouldn't treat my brand-new mower like that. She should at least put it under cover. She must realise what she is doing. I never should have let her borrow it!*

See the shoulds? See what they are up to? Busily fermenting the following responses: resentment, disappointment, frustration, anger.

You see, you have a belief that if you do something nice for someone they will repay the favour, and treat your possessions the way you would. *This does not always happen*. Like a colleague of mine once said, 'The planet where human beings do what you think they should is not this one.'

A few tips

1. Get rid of the 'shoulds' from your thinking—they're not considered a thought virus for nothing. Replace them with words that are less demanding. Clients have often told me that if the only thing they took from therapy was to stop using the word 'should', they were happy—they felt liberated.

2. In terms of alternative words, look for words that emphasise choice.

For example, instead of thinking, *I should do all of the housework today, it has to be done and it must be done today*—which sounds like time for a cup of tea and a lie-down with the raging headache you've just given yourself—try thinking this way: *I could do the housework today. But I've had a big week, so I might do some today and leave the rest for tomorrow.*

Now, doesn't that feel better?

Well, that's enough for today. For this week's homework I'd like you to fill out the thought record on the next page.

A	B	C	D
A SITUATION	B THOUGHTS	C FEELINGS	D THOUGHT VIRUSES
		C BIOLOGY	
		C BEHAVIOUR	

This is similar to the last thought record, but this time you will notice the extra column for the thought viruses.

Just like before, describe the event (A), then write down all your thoughts (B), then your responses (C). Don't forget to rate the units of distress. Then, in the final column, I want you to go back to the B column and find the thought viruses, then write them down in column D.

The event can be anything you like. Try to find a time in the past week when you have been distressed at 70% or over. The need for this high level is because we are trying to target what causes you the most discomfort.

Do the best you can. See you next time.

(I must admit I'd be intrigued to know what you would do if I asked to borrow the lawn mower a second time.)

CHAPTER NINE

THE THOUGHT DIARY

Me: Nice to see you back. How's the couch?

You: When I went over what we did last time I realised that I was **catastrophising** with a **negative filter**. Then once I started **emotional reasoning**, I started to believe that I was in the right and she was in the wrong (**cognitive reasoning**). Once I realised I had made it all up in my mind, I apologised for over-reacting and I'm back home.

Me: Well done. Did you go through what you had learned with your partner?

You: Yeah, I did. I showed her the list of thought viruses, and it gave her a good understanding of how I was thinking. She doesn't think like me, so it came as a bit of a surprise.

Me: It's a really helpful idea to share what you are learning. Because, as you pointed out, not everybody thinks in the same way.

Couples and mind-reading

Couples are very prone to assuming that they think the same as each other. When more often than not it occurs as described above: *My partner had no idea what I was thinking, because she thinks differently than I do.*

If two people assume that they think the same, communications are frequently cross-wired, and conflicts and stalemates are a common outcome.

Let me explain:

You arrive home from work and see your partner sitting in the lounge, gazing out the window. No hello, and when you say, 'Hi, how's your day been?', no reply.

> **You:** Is everything OK—you don't seem yourself?
> **Partner:** Perfectly fine. Thanks for asking.

You: So everything's fine?

Partner: Yes, I said.

You: (still a little uncertain, but taking things at face value, because you're not a mind-reader) Cool, OK then, everything's OK. Well, in that case I think I might go out for a few beers with the boys.

Partner: You bastard!! Do what you like!!

I bet he's forgotten this is the anniversary of the day we met.

It's the boss's birthday—if everything is cool at home I think I'll join the gang for a celebratory drink.

I'm sure most of you have been through a similar situation. But no matter how long you have been with someone, familiarity does not mean either of you are mind-readers. Acting on assumptions is not only unhelpful, it is potentially very destructive.

Now, before we get started on your new thought record, I've gone through the first sheet you did for me and identified the thought viruses. Now that you are integrating the language and new information, this will make more sense.

A	B	C	D

A SITUATION

Email memo sent round at work. Restructure meeting set for Thursday.

B THOUGHTS

Oh no, this is it. I'm going to be fired.
The boss thinks I'm redundant. They are all planning to get me fired.
What if I never get another job?
I'm of no use to my family.

C FEELINGS

Upset, sad, fearful (90%)

C BIOLOGY

Heart racing, shallow breathing, butterflies in the stomach

C BEHAVIOUR

Avoiding the phone, worrying, pacing

D THOUGHT VIRUSES

magnification, fortune-telling, negative mental filter, mind-reading, emotional reasoning, labelling, overgeneralising

You: OK . . . I found quite a few thought viruses myself. No wonder I get myself in such a state.

Me: I want to take you through this thought record one column at a time, and not only highlight for you the varying thought viruses but also explain how they impact on you, and discuss a few techniques to reattribute the meanings you are giving this event.

A: You're informed of a restructuring meeting.

B: You instantly begin to 'worry'. This is what your thoughts are telling you.

$$\downarrow$$

Oh no, this is it. I'm going to be fired.

So the memo is immediately **catastrophised**, and in a very **all-or-nothing** manner you tell yourself that everything is over—the job, your future and so on.

You are totally convinced (90%) that you're going to be fired. You have discovered this information by putting on your **'fortune-telling'** hat. You have also, through the filter of **personalisation**, proven to yourself that the memo was in fact directed at you, and only you. It was emailed as an office memo only to disguise the fact, that you, and only you (in your mind), are going to be fired.

The boss thinks I'm redundant.

Now here's evidence of your **mind-reading** abilities. In the thought above you have already read the future—but now you can read people's minds. Now that's gifted!

However, where this thought really gains its devilish power is once you start **cognitive reasoning**. You now start to believe (90%) that what you are thinking is based in fact. This can never be true, because you are believing a thought that is a result of mind-reading—and therefore non-factual.

They are all planning to get me fired.

Here we go again! Dysfunctional thinking in the lead, rational thinking coming in a definite last. You are now **mind-reading** in groups—you know what everyone (**all-or-nothing**) in your office is thinking. But wait, there's more . . .

You know what they will be thinking *in the future* (**fortune-telling**) and it will be seen through a **negative filter**.

I can't believe how upset, sad and fearful I am feeling right now (90%), just writing down these thoughts, and I don't even believe this shit!

↓

What if I never get another job?

And here it is: the worry mantra—what if?

(A little reminder of the definition of worry—the prediction of negative catastrophic outcomes.)

The prediction is, in this instance, that you *will never again* in your life get another job and that will be a complete **catastrophe** (90%).

You'll be feeling pretty miserable by now and that is not surprising, believing all this unsubstantiated crap. So I now look to the C column and observe the racing heart, shallow breathing and butterflies in the stomach, registering at 90%. You're really getting distressed.

Round about now **emotional reasoning** has attached to all of the other thought distortions and you now believe everything that you are feeling and the biological sensations (**biological reasoning**).

I'm of no use to my family.

No more making jokes. This thinking is scary and is the type of thinking that contributes to and co-exists with depressive mood and depressive illness. We are at the very end of what is known as a thought chain.

N.B. You will have noticed that I have placed arrows between each thought. We call this the 'downward arrow technique'—remarkably enough. Clinicians track the chain of thoughts down to where your most painful thoughts reside, and work with those. Christine Padesky (author of *Mind Over Mood*) calls this a 'hot thought'. It's the one that upsets you the most—the one that *believing* in is the most painful for you.

I emphasise the words 'believe'
and 'believing' because they
are concepts fundamental
to the workings and success
of cognitive therapy.

Let me explain:

On your thought record, in the emotional and biological response section you rated SUDS at 90%—very powerful negative subjective experiences. These are your 'affectual responses'. (Affect—pronounced *aff*-ect—is a concept used in psychology to describe the experience of feeling or emotion.)

Very often, that 90% can subside by doing a little breathing technique (see page 230) or implementing one of your most important skills for the time ahead:

Identify the thought viruses and
question the existence or non-
existence of facts in your thinking.

Here are a few examples—I'm sure you'll think of others.

- Mind-reading: I cannot mind-read—**fact**
- Predicting disaster: I am not a fortune-teller—**fact**
- Personalising: Not everything is about me—**fact**

I cannot emphasise enough the importance of memorising the list of thought viruses (see page 251)—otherwise your skills are not portable.

It may well be that you have catastrophised everything and you don't feel that you can attempt to rationalise your thoughts. However, it is very important that you *learn to manage these situations*.

Here is a very immediate and impactful technique. We'll go through it and then I will explain to you how to implement the strategy:

In your mind, head back to both of us in my office. I ask you to imagine going outside and switching your phone back on after the session. You see a 'Please call home urgently' text.

You call straight away, and are informed that someone you love dearly has been hit on a pedestrian crossing by a truck, and is in Accident & Emergency.

I then ask you to rate the experience of receiving that news.

> **You:** That would be a 100%!!
>
> **Me:** Hang on just a moment—he/she is still alive and you don't know whether things are critical.
>
> **You:** True—I just felt so terrified. OK, then. Well, I'd rate this at 95%.
>
> **Me:** That's fine. Now, here is the technique.

'THE TERRIBLENESS SCALE' FOR DECATASTROPHISING

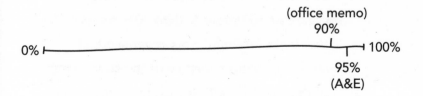

Me: I can tell by the look on your face that you're a little embarrassed and awkward, seeing the close proximity (5%) between the two events. So, to give you an opportunity to redeem yourself—so to speak—I'll ask if you would like to change the rating of the office memo.

You: I would move it to 30%—I mean, it wasn't like I wasn't pissed off . . .

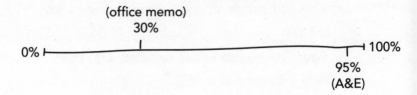

(office memo)
30%

0% ——————————————————— 100%

95%
(A&E)

Me: Well done—that was a fabulous shift of 60 units of distress. At a rating of 50 units of distress and below, your subjective, physical and emotional states become easier to manage and you are again becoming equipped to rationally think, *Oh yes, doesn't that feel a lot better.* This lower score of 30% is far more reflective of the seriousness of the situation with the office memo.

The 90% rating was nothing more than an example of you scaring yourself, with your distorted thoughts all based in fiction, not fact, mirroring negative and unhelpful perceptions of reality.

Now, take out a piece of white card and draw what's below on it. Or of course you can do this on your phone if you have drawing tools:

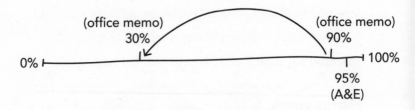

(office memo) 30%
(office memo) 90%
0% ⊢ ⊣ 100%
95% (A&E)

Now, at the bottom of the card I want you to write the following:

How bad is this really?

This question asks you: 'In the real world, how terrible is this situation?'

The use of a technique such as this is akin to having a perspective scale. In a very tangible format, it highlights for you what is *really* important.

As you can see, this is a very impactful method for 'coming down' from being highly distressed. It is certainly a bit uncomfortable at the beginning of the visualisation, but then discomfort never killed anybody. I believe it's worth the discomfort for the benefits.

I realise there are a few loose ends still from this session, regarding the importance of 'believe' and 'believability'. However, we have covered enough material for now. Let's save the rest for next time.

Homework

Once again, make another thought record. Don't bother with column D for now—that's part of next week's session. Just fill it out the same as previously.

See you next time, and well done on the 'decatastrophising'.

A	B	C
A SITUATION	**B THOUGHTS**	**C FEELINGS**
		C BIOLOGY
		C BEHAVIOUR

CHAPTER TEN

STARTING TO SEE RESULTS

Me: Hi there, you're looking pleased with yourself. How's it going?

You: Really good—I even struggled with what I was going to put on my thought record. Nothing seemed to bother me as much as usual.

Me: A bit of decatastrophising, perhaps?

You: Certainly have been. I showed everyone at home how it worked. They thought it was cool. Even my teenagers were saying things like, 'Wow, it's like my problems aren't really that big.'

I have been using it if I feel overwhelmed, but that doesn't seem to be happening as much, either. I am tending to *think* more rather than just reacting to things and letting rather trivial events get the better of me.

The other thing I have been doing is paying more conscious attention to what is going on in my thinking. Like, the other day, I started to think that my friends were ignoring me and were thinking I was too high-maintenance to be friends with. Then I realised that I was mind-reading and told myself quickly that I wasn't, in fact, a mind-reader. It worked.

Me: Cool. Right—let's have a look at that thought record.

A	B	C
A SITUATION Got invitation to my high-school reunion.	**B THOUGHTS** What if they think I have put on weight and that I'm fat? I'll get there and they will all be really happy and successful, and have really expensive clothes. What if no one will talk to me because I'm so boring and I never know what to say? I'll get so embarrassed my face will turn red, and everyone will notice and think I look like a traffic light on legs. Then I'll say something stupid and won't be able to breathe, and then I'll panic. I definitely shouldn't go. It will be a disaster.	**C FEELINGS** nervous, useless, embarrassed, stupid, afraid (75%) **C BIOLOGY** tense, anxious, shallow breathing, heart racing, butterflies in the stomach **C BEHAVIOUR** hid the letter, avoided Facebook and Instagram, started to worry

You: I did manage to get my anxiety from nearly 100 down to 75%, but thinking about going to the reunion just kept going around and around in my head. Like that spiral, I couldn't seem to stop the worry.

Me: First of all, you haven't failed. As I commented earlier, worry is very slippery and stubborn. It's a lifetime habit that won't go overnight.

Because this is almost our last session, I'm going to utilise this final thought record as a vehicle to provide you with more knowledge and skills.

A: SITUATION. Got invitation to my high-school reunion.

So, in the real world, you received an invitation.

C: FEELINGS. Nervous, useless, embarrassed, stupid, afraid. SUDS: 75%

C: BIOLOGY. Tense, anxious, shallow breathing, heart racing, butterflies in the stomach

C: BEHAVIOUR. Hid the letter, avoided Facebook and Instagram, started to worry

Like clockwork, you started to worry, and experience the distressing emotional and biological effects. This is called 'anticipatory anxiety' created by worry—anxiety in anticipation of an event. Once again, all created by your imagination.

Then you tried to avoid the stimulus (invitation), by hiding it in a drawer, where no one could see it and ask you about it.

Actions like these are called 'safety behaviours'. You are trying to keep your anxiety down by staying away from the trigger. This will perhaps work in the short term, but that's all. The counter-productive aspect of this strategy is that you maintain the belief that the trigger is to be feared and avoided.

It is the *meaning* you are attaching to the invitation that is causing you the distress. So let's have a look at the cognitive processing.

B: THOUGHTS. **What if they think** I have put on weight and **that I'm fat?**

I'll get there and **they will all** be really happy and successful, and have really expensive clothes.

What if no one will talk to me because **I'm so boring** and I **never** know what to say?

I'll get so embarrassed my face **will turn** red, and **everyone will** notice and **think** I look like a traffic light on legs.

Then **I'll say** something **stupid** and **won't be able** to breathe, and **then I'll** panic.

I definitely **shouldn't** go. It **will** be a disaster.

Me: Your turn to play 'spot the thought viruses'. Just go through one thought at a time.

You: The first thing I notice is the What ifs?, so immediately I know I am predicting negative events. Heaps of mind-reading: 'they will think . . .', which because of the 'will' is fortune-telling. The whole lot is seen through a negative filter. All-or-nothing thinking; no one, everyone, they will all. The themes of emotional, biological and cognitive reasoning are all there, convincing me that everything I'm thinking is true. Finished off with a 'shouldn't' and an 'I can't stand it, I'm not going!'

Me: Fantastic! Very cool. Now I am going to introduce a format for taking all of this highly irrational thinking and reattributing the meaning so that the thoughts are rational. I call it . . . the cognitive matrix.

A MATRIX FOR CHALLENGING IRRATIONAL THOUGHTS

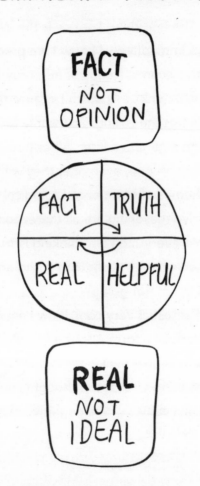

To achieve rational thinking, ask yourself:
Is my thinking based in fact, truth
and reality? Is my thinking helpful?

A MATRIX FOR CHALLENGING IRRATIONAL THOUGHTS

Rational thinking is based in fact, truth, and what is real and helpful. Irrational thoughts are based in opinions and ideals.

Thinking you can mind-read and predict the future is **not based in fact**.

Knowing that they will all be happy and successful is **not true**, because again you are looking into the future.

How can any of these thoughts be based in what is **real** when none of them are based in **fact**? They are projections of your irrational thinking.

If it was **true** that as soon as you arrived, a group of your old classmates came over and said, 'F@ck, have you put on weight!', I could hardly accuse you of predictive mind-reading. What I would ask you, however, is, 'How **helpful** is it for you to play those thoughts around and around in your head?'

When you **imagined** they would be noticing how much weight you had put on, and that you were clinically obese, even if it was **true** that they were thinking that, is that **fact** or is it their **opinion**?

Also, don't forget that 99 per cent of the time people are thinking about themselves not you.

Let's go back to the imaginary reunion. You get there and they will all be really happy, wearing their hugely expensive clothes, dripping with enough diamonds to feed a developing country. Then you, looking directly into their thoughts with a gut feeling, notice that they think **you should** have done much better with your life, and certainly **should not** have let yourself go.

By feeling inadequate you are believing that their values and beliefs and ideals are what is really important and that you have failed.

That you **should** be like them is believing that their ideals are the *right* ones and what you believe is *wrong*. Bullshit! If you enjoy your reality, then who cares what other people think? (Not that you know what they are thinking.)

Also remember: 'Comparison is the thief of joy' —THEODORE ROOSEVELT

You can see how the 'cognitive matrix' provides you with a model to evaluate your thinking and determine what is irrational versus rational. Your goal is to stick with what is rational and helpful.

BELIEVE IT OR NOT!

We've talked a lot about beliefs, values and ideals in this session; about how opinions are not facts, and that what other people think you 'should' be doing has to do with their ideals and nothing to do with your reality.

On the subject of beliefs, it's probably time I explained what that 'believe and believability' thing that I mentioned earlier means.

> **Me:** Let's go back to your thought record. You recorded 75 out of 100 units of distress thinking about the reunion. You also noted down thoughts about being fat and stupid. Now that we have gone through rationalising those thoughts, how do you feel?
> **You:** Much more relaxed—probably only

about 30 units of discomfort.

Me: OK. Now how much do you still believe, on a scale of 1 to 10, that you are fat and boring?

You: 7 out of 10. That hasn't changed much at all, because that's how I feel about myself.

Therein lies the struggle. Challenging your thoughts can shift the *affect*—the intensity of your responses. Shifting that 'believability' factor, on the other hand, is complex work, because it links to the fundamental beliefs you have about yourself.

Before we wind up, let me provide you with some insight into how to take your irrational thoughts and find rational alternatives. Have a look at the table on the next page.

IRRATIONAL	RATIONAL
What if they think I have put on weight and that I'm fat?	I hope I'm not surrounded by a whole lot of judgemental people.
I'll get there and they will all be really happy and successful, and have really expensive clothes.	It's only a reunion—I don't have to know what people are doing with their lives.
What if I get there and no one will talk to me because I'm so boring and I never know what to say?	If people don't talk to me I won't stay long.
Then I'll get so embarrassed my face will turn red, and everyone will notice and think I look like a traffic light on legs.	I'm sure I won't be the only person there feeling a bit shy and awkward and maybe a tad embarrassed.
Then I'll say something stupid and won't be able to breathe, and then I'll panic.	If I do feel short of breath I'll just wander off and do my breathing exercises. People will be so busy talking about whatever, they're hardly likely to be looking to see if I have left the room to have a panic attack.
I definitely shouldn't go. It will be a disaster.	Why not go—what's the worst that could happen?

Feel a bit more comfortable?

If you're spooked about an event that is coming up (suffering from *anticipatory anxiety*), write down your thoughts on your most recent thought record. Then create rational alternative thoughts the way I have above, and watch those units of distress dissipate.

Time to finish. No homework for next time. We'll just review what you have in your cognitive toolkit and add just a few more strategies, for when you're out there independently managing your internal world.

CHAPTER ELEVEN

TIME TO REVIEW

Me: Well, today's our last get-together, so I would like to review how you are getting on utilising what you have learned so far.

You: I'm feeling so much more in control of my thoughts and feelings. The **decatastrophising** and getting rid of the **'should/must/have to'** thoughts are the main tools I implement. These really help me to stay calmer and not blow things out of proportion, or get resentful and angry if things don't go the way I believe they **'should'**.

I am able to communicate more effectively in my relationships, by avoiding **mind-reading** and **fortune-telling** in particular. With my partner I use the list of thought viruses to work through what may have just happened in the miscommunication.

Knowing what **emotional and cognitive reasoning** are, and how they affect my perception, slows me down so that I am not reacting based on emotion. I pause, take a few breaths, then look for the evidence, asking myself, 'Is this reaction based in fact?'

I use the **'cognitive matrix'** to help with this process of rationalising my thoughts, to keep them based in fact.

The area where I get most stuck is trying to get out of that **'worrisome overthinking spiral'**. So, I would like a few more strategies for that.

Me: No problem. I haven't as yet explained thoroughly to you the variety of uses for flashcards.

RETRAINING THE BRAIN USING FLASHCARDS

Research tells us that if you are wanting to change the way you think, you need to internalise effectively the new way of thinking. By doing that you have more chance of replacing the old thinking habits.

On page 192 I showed you using the **'How bad is this really?'** statement on a card, to help you decatastrophise. This enables you to reduce your arousal level, so you are able to manage the emotional overload more effectively.

With worry, as you are aware, you start with the **'what if?'**, which then takes you into the prediction (**fortune-telling**) of negative (**negative filter**) catastrophic outcomes (**magnification**).

Emotional/biological and cognitive reasoning convince you that your distorted thoughts are telling you the truth. You have tried thinking 'stop worrying' and ended up thinking about camels.

The priority here is to get out of the loop as quickly as possible. For this purpose there are flashcards.

For flashcards to be effective, you must look at them a few times per day for a minimum of 15 seconds. There is no point picking them up, or looking at your phone, then five seconds later discarding the new thought. You need to carve new tracks in the brain and a quick glance will *not* achieve this.

These two in particular I have found very successful:

HOW IS THIS THINKING HELPING ME/YOU?

WHERE IS THIS THINKING TAKING ME/YOU?

You will notice I have provided a choice of pronouns—I leave it up to you which is the most powerful for you, when you are internally talking to yourself (thinking).

I would also like you to notice that, unlike 'stop worrying about . . .', these flashcards make use of questioning: 'How?' and 'Where?' These are two of the questions used in Socratic dialogue, the backbone of law and cognitive therapy (the other two questions being 'When?' and 'What?'. I don't use the 'Why' question, as I don't find it helpful—it sends the brain on a different mission that is very rarely solution-focused.)

Finally, I have reached an area of neuroscience that I know very little about—in fact, nothing! However, what I do know, anecdotally, is that when you ask the brain one of these questions, it goes looking for the correct answer. Socrates referred to this as 'guided discovery'.

In cognitive therapy it is defined as:

A process that a therapist uses to help his or her client reflect on the way that they process information. Through the processes of answering questions or reflecting on thinking processes, a range of alternative thinking is opened up for each client.

So when you ask the brain, 'How is this thinking (worrying) helping you?', the answer is spontaneously, 'It's not.' The brain then concurs with the questioning. Therefore, the worrying is not suppressed and squashed—it is challenged. This is a big difference, and not such an internal battle.

HEY CAMEL ... IT'S PRETTY SQUISHED IN HERE...

See pages 241-249 for some flashcards to cut out and use, or type these messages into your phone, so you have them at hand.

WORRY DELAY

This next technique is taken from 'worry delay' research. Some theorists suggest the following (which by all means feel free to try):

You set aside a worry time every evening, say at 6 p.m., for no less than 30 minutes. Then you sit down for uninterrupted worry time. No phone, no screens, no conversation—nothing but worry. (Ah, bliss!) During this time, you write down everything you are worrying about in a notebook.

So when you're at work and you start to worry about a project, you think to yourself, *I'm not going to worry right now, but will save it for my worry time when I get home.* The rationale behind this strategy is that your brain is told that it can worry—but just a bit later in the day.

In the days that follow, you start to notice a couple of phenomena. Firstly, you get bored and somewhat irritated with the worrying exercise, wishing it would end. Secondly, looking back over your notes, you observe that the things you were worrying about two days ago you can hardly even remember.

Hence, you have essentially 'flooded' the brain with worry, increasingly experiencing the futility of the exercise and the futility of worry.

This is a time-consuming exercise and I work with very few people who can actually be bothered doing it, so if that is how you feel you're not alone.

Anyway, borrowing from this approach I designed another flashcard:

NOT NOW!!

I have borrowed from the worry-delay approach, but have utilised only the essence of the approach in this flashcard.

'Not now' still requires the brain to delay the worrying, while promising the opportunity to worry later, working on a gratification-delay method. A client of mine who found 'not now' a very useful technique described it this way:

It reminds me of when I was about four years old, out with my parents and officiously demanding an ice cream. I remember, when I was told 'not now', it occurred to me that I was going to get an ice cream but just not straight away. I also worked out that if I slowed down the bad behaviour, this could bring the ice cream even closer.

This is what 'not now' tells your brain. You want to worry because you believe that it will help relieve your anxiety. So by being told to 'wait to worry' you know you will eventually get to relieve the anxiety. Again, this approach subtly demonstrates that worry does not change the outcome, and that continuing to worry does nothing more than 'clutter' your brain.

The limits of consciousness

So often we credit the brain with limitless power, believing that the magnificence of the organism (us) is infinite. Certainly, when you read anything about DNA and its intricate complexity, it is easy to assume that this also applies to the consciousness.

However, this does not apply to *conscious processing*. Things have to be in order and structured. There cannot be too many things going on or the brain starts to get confused.

For example, if I talk to you one on one, your concentration is stable. Put another person in the room talking and concentration gets a little more difficult, and one more person talking and it's 'all over, Rover'.

Hence, fill the brain with too much worrying and negative mind-wandering, and the ability to attend, concentrate and produce becomes impaired, because there is only so much room in the conscious brain. So do yourself a favour and avoid the clutter of 'worrisome overthinking'.

CONCERN AND WORRY

Concern and *worry* are different. The circular pattern of worry, as you know by now, achieves nothing. Concern, on the other hand, has specific destinations in mind: time-frames, solutions, action plans. For instance, concern can assist with:

- planning to minimise the impact of, or hopefully avoid, the feared situation occurring
- putting steps into place and action plans for if and when it does
- making lists of time-frames, perhaps thinking of who can help and what needs to be done.

Use the word *concern* not worry. Thinking 'I am *concerned* about something' to me immediately infers subsequent action, e.g. problem-solving.

A WORRY MANAGEMENT TECHNIQUE

The diagram opposite provides you with an immediate tool to structure your ruminative thinking (worry).

By using this chart you can create an action plan. Write things down and let them go. This is especially good for work-related issues. Keep a copy of it beside your bed so if you wake in the night you can record your thoughts and solutions and go back to sleep!

DISTRACTION

The other important part of this chart is the use of distraction. In both the fields of chronic pain management and worrisome overthinking, distraction is one of the most powerful techniques there is. If you can, think about something different or do something different. Remember the old adage: 'Take your mind off things'.

WORRY DECISION MAP

The Worry Decision Map is a structured way of solving the worry problem. It is a way of asking yourself a branching series of questions that help to let the worry drop.

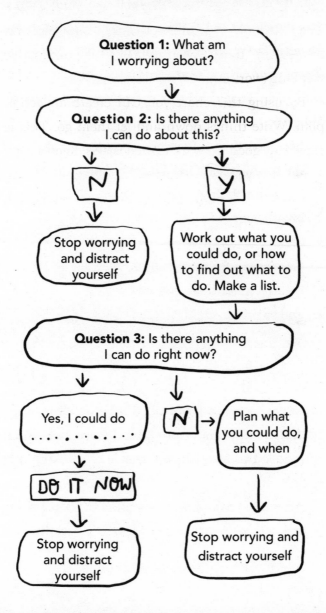

BREATHING

When you are feeling anxious it can really help if you remember to breathe. That sounds a bit crazy, because we're always breathing, right? But what happens when you're anxious is that you can tend to hold your breath and this makes everything worse. When you feel like that, try this:

- hold your breath for six counts (don't make the mistake of taking a deep breath and hyperventilating)
- breathe out
- breathe in for three counts
- breathe out for three counts
- breathe in for three counts
- and so on . . .

AND FINALLY, HELPFUL THINKING

We have spoken a lot about thinking that is based in fact, reality and truth. But I have not as yet introduced you to the importance of thinking that is 'helpful'.

After I had a double mastectomy in 2009, I wrote a book called *Breast Support* (essential reading for women who have just been diagnosed with breast cancer). In that book I wrote a chapter on 'How to get off the worry roundabout', which discussed the importance of 'helpful' thinking. I would like to again plagiarise my work, and I quote:

This wonderful word 'helpful' reminds me of the Red Cross symbol. It is recognised globally as a symbol of people helping people. Only terrorists and extremists show no respect for it, because of their fanatical belief systems.

The word 'helpful' is not about making judgements, it's not based on shoulds or shouldn'ts, and nor does it make statements about what's normal or abnormal, right or wrong.

So even if something does go wrong, or someone does say something nasty about you, ask yourself about the *value* of ruminating on these thoughts. Remember to think:

'How is this thinking helping me?'

Well, that's it. I hope you have found all of this information 'helpful'.

The Book of Overthinking is not an alternative to therapy, but for those of you who perhaps cannot afford therapy, are not within close proximity to clinical psychologists, or just want to try to do it on your own, this book will provide a good in-road into managing your intrusive and worrisome overthinking.

If it has made no difference, I suggest you seek professional psychological help, as your anxiety may be the result of some other condition.

All the best—it's been great working with you.

NAMASTE

233

IMPORTANT STUFF
TO REMEMBER

1. The head is attached to the shoulders. Hence all the different components that make us who we are—biology, behaviour, emotions and cognitions—are inextricably linked. These connections work for both the negative and the positive aspects of your world.

2. Worrying by definition is when you consistently make negative, catastrophic predictions about the future.

3. Overthinking is a problem 'when it is thinking that gets in the way of your ability to function' (Dr R. Shieff).

4. Theorists estimate a 25 to 40 per cent genetic influence/contribution to anxiety.

5. There is no point telling a worrier to 'just stop worrying'.

6. When children witness the behaviour of worry, they start to believe that to worry is important—because it is what the grown-ups do, it must really be important and vital to adult survival.

7. It is very clear in the research that 'worrisome overthinking' has long-term effects on mood, and one very strong connection is with depression.

8. Worry is a superstitious behaviour. It has neither predictive nor preventative power.

9. 'What if?' If you notice these two words together in your thinking, shut them down as soon as you can—distract, use a flashcard. It is only the never-ending downward spiral at work once again.

10. Your anxiety can be triggered both internally and externally. A thought can switch your entire system into a fearful alert mode (panic).

11. Changing *how* you think is the key.

12. Don't forget the skill of 'reattribution of meaning'. Your perception is not the same as reality.

13. A = Reality (this is *not* the problem)
B = Thinking/cognition (this is where therapy mostly occurs)
C = Responses: emotions/biology/behaviour (this is where the problems lie)

14. Irrational thoughts create exaggerated emotions because you believe them to be true.

15. The brain can and does lie to you. The **thought viruses** allow this to happen. So, you must memorise them!! (Refer to Appendix 2, page 251.)

16. Share what you are learning with those close to you so they get familiar with the language—in particular, the thought viruses.

17. No matter how much you love someone, you cannot read their mind and they cannot read yours.

18. Decatatsrophising is a quick and easy method for calming yourself down. Don't forget to use the 'terribleness scale'.

19. Rational thinking is based in fact, truth, and what is real and helpful.

20. Irrational thoughts are based in opinions and ideals. Stick with the rational!

21. Being concerned is far more preferable than worrying.

APPENDIX 1

FLASHCARDS

I CAN'T CHANGE REALITY,
BUT I CAN CHANGE HOW I
THINK ABOUT REALITY BY
CHANGING HOW I THINK.

- - - - - - - - - - - - - - -

SOMETHING FALSE CAN FEEL VERY
TRUE. I MUSTN'T LET A FEELING
CONVINCE ME IT'S A FACT.

- - - - - - - - - - - - - - -

PERCEIVED THREATS ARE
NOT LIFE-THREATENING.

- - - - - - - - - - - - - - -

WHERE IS THIS THINKING
TAKING ME?

HOW IS THIS THINKING
HELPING ME?

- -

HOW IS MY THINKING TRUE?

- -

FEELINGS ARE NOT FACTS.
BELIEFS ARE NOT FACTS.

- -

DISCOMFORT MAY BE
UNCOMFORTABLE, BUT IT
WON'T KILL ME. JUST
BREATHE AND RIDE IT OUT.

- -

NOT NOW!

I'M SCARING MYSELF WITH
MY OWN THOUGHTS.

- - - - - - - - - - - - - - -

WORRYING DOES NOTHING
EXCEPT CAUSE DISTRESS.

- - - - - - - - - - - - - - -

WORRY IS SUPERSTITIOUS
BEHAVIOUR.

- - - - - - - - - - - - - - -

THE TERRIBLENESS SCALE:
0%————————————100%
HOW BAD IS THIS REALLY?

FACT VS. OPINION

REAL VS. IDEAL

TRUE/HELPFUL

APPENDIX 2

THOUGHT VIRUSES

All-or-nothing thinking: The world is seen in very black-and-white terms, using words like always/never, nobody/everybody, everything/nothing. A very rigid way of thinking.

Biological reasoning: When you rush to assume that a physical sensation is a sign that something *really bad* must be happening to you (e.g. brain tumour, gum cancer).

Catastrophising: *see* **Magnification**.

Cognitive reasoning: Very similar to its counterpart thought virus **emotional reasoning**. The assumption that because you think and even perhaps believe something to be true, then it must be so.

Disqualifying the positive: Not only focusing on the negative, but also filtering out anything positive that you may have achieved.

Emotional reasoning: Convincing yourself that because you feel something it *must* be a fact.

Fortune-telling: Constantly predicting negative outcomes.

'I can't stand its': When you tell yourself that you literally cannot stand another minute, another word, another day, and start to believe it to be true.

Jumping to conclusions: The foundation of assumptions based on no evidence, with negative interpretations stemming solely from your own beliefs. The two elements to this thought virus are **mind-reading** and **fortune-telling**.

Labelling: Overgeneralising, but as well as picking out what you did wrong, also springing into negative self-talk (e.g. 'I always make this same mistake, I'm such a f@ckwit!').

Magnification, AKA catastrophising: When a molehill becomes a mountain. You exaggerate and exaggerate problems and don't stop until you are exhausted from being overwhelmed.

Mind-reading: When you arbitrarily, based on a whim, conclude that people are thinking negatively about you, without any evidence that this is true.

Minimisation: Magnification in reverse. You take the mountains (e.g. your significant achievements) and shrink them into molehills. By doing so you get to avoid acknowledging your strengths and desirable qualities.

Moralistic 'shoulds': shoulds, musts and have tos based on values, beliefs and expectations—not facts (as opposed to instructional 'shoulds', which are helpful).

Negative mental filter: The tendency to see only the negative and dark side of life.

Overgeneralisation: One unpleasant event is seen as a never-ending pattern of defeat.

Personalisation: The belief that you are the cause of external events that you have nothing to do with, or that you were not primarily responsible for.

Shoulds, musts and have tos: These words all mean the same and hence create the same emotional, biological and behavioural responses. They are all control-based words, used through the centuries to govern through guilt. Toxic! Do yourself a favour and get rid of them!

Make sure you memorise these thought viruses so you know how to spot them, and address them!

THOUGHT RECORDS

A	B	C	D
A SITUATION	B THOUGHTS	C FEELINGS	D THOUGHT VIRUSES
		C BIOLOGY	
		C BEHAVIOUR	

A	B	C	D
A SITUATION	B THOUGHTS	C FEELINGS	D THOUGHT VIRUSES
		C BIOLOGY	
		C BEHAVIOUR	

A	B	C	D
A SITUATION	B THOUGHTS	C FEELINGS	D THOUGHT VIRUSES
		C BIOLOGY	
		C BEHAVIOUR	

A	B	C	D
A SITUATION	B THOUGHTS	C FEELINGS	D THOUGHT VIRUSES
		C BIOLOGY	
		C BEHAVIOUR	

FURTHER READING

Burns, Dr David, *Feeling Good: The New Mood Therapy*, HarperCollins, 2011.

LeDoux, Dr Joseph, *The Emotional Brain*, Orion, 2004.

Mayer, Dr Emeran, *The Mind-Gut Connection: How the Hidden Conversation Within Our Bodies Impacts Our Mood, Our Choices, and Our Overall Health*, HarperCollins, 2016.

Padesky, Dr Christine, *Mind Over Mood*, Guilford Press, 2015.

Wegner, Dr Daniel M., *White Bears and Other Unwanted Thoughts*, Guilford Press, 1994.

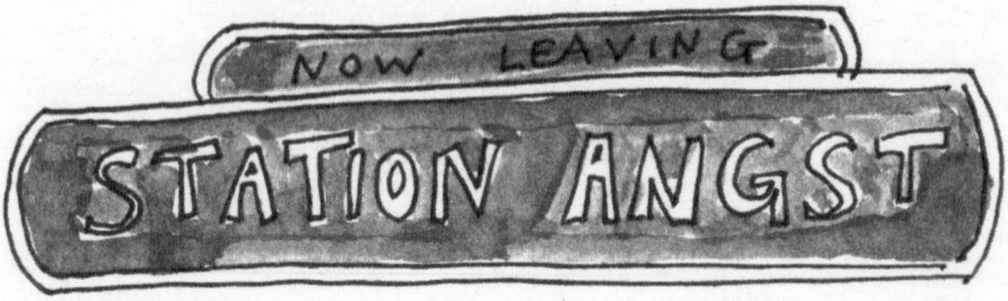
NOW LEAVING
STATION ANGST